Global Entrepreneurship Monitor India Report 2020/21

A National Study on Entrepreneurship

Global Entrepreneurship Monitor India Report 2020/21

A National Study on Entrepreneurship

Authored by

Sunil Shukla
Director-General Entrepreneurship Development Institute of India

Pankaj Bharti
Assistant Professor, Entrepreneurship Development Institute of India

Amit Kumar Dwivedi
Associate Professor, Entrepreneurship Development Institute of India

First published 2022
by CRC Press
2 Park Square, Milton Park, Abingdon, Oxon, OX14 4RN

and by Routledge
52 Vanderbilt Avenue, New York, NY 10017

Routledge is an imprint of the Taylor & Francis Group, an Informa business

British Library Cataloguing-in-Publication Data
A catalogue record for this book is available from the British Library

ISBN: 978-1-032-22417-6 (pbk)

Table of Contents

List of Figures

List of Tables

Author's Profile

Sunil Shukla (Ph.D., Psychology)
Director General
Entrepreneurship Development Institute of India
National Team Leader, GEM India
Email: sunilshukla@ediindia.org

Dr. Sunil Shukla, Director General of Entrepreneurship Development Institute of India, Ahmedabad, has been closely working, for more than three decades now, in entrepreneurship education, research, training and institution building. Dr. Shukla has envisioned and designed innovative, outcome based programmes and developmental interventions in the domains of 'entrepreneurship', 'start ups' and 'intrapreneurship' for varied target groups including potential & existing entrepreneurs, innovators, faculty, business executives, bankers, managers, disadvantaged sections, family business successors, administrators and business counsellors. An entrepreneurship exponent, Dr. Shukla's work has also left an indelible impact on the grounds of Greater Mekong Subregion (GMS) countries, Asia, Africa, America, Iran and Uzbekistan. His research work has led to notable policy advocacy and decisions. He leads the largest and the most prestigious annual study of entrepreneurial dynamics in the world – the *Global Entrepreneurship Monitor (GEM) India Chapter*. Today several organizations and departments are benefitting from his guidance and mentorship by having him on their Boards.

Pankaj Bharti (Ph.D. Psychology)
Assistant Professor
Entrepreneurship Development Institute of India
National Team Member, GEM India
Email: pbharti@ediindia.org

Dr. Pankaj Bharti specialises in Organisational Behaviour, Human Resource Management and Corporate Entrepreneurship. He is trained in conceptualising and developing measurement tools for social science research. He holds more than 14 years of experience in academics and industry. He is associated with over 20 National as well as international research projects. He is also a National Team Member of Global Entrepreneurship Monitor (GEM), India and he is co-author of GEM India Report 2014, 2015/16, 2016/17, 2017/18, 2018/19 and 2019/20. His core competency lies in psychometric assessment administration and reporting.

Amit Kumar Dwivedi (Ph.D., Commerce)
Associate Professor
Entrepreneurship Development Institute of India
National Team Member, GEM India
Email: akdwivedi@ediindia.org

Dr. Amit Kumar Dwivedi has over 16 years of teaching and research experience. He has earned a doctoral degree in Industrial Finance from Lucknow University. His areas of interest are Entrepreneurship Education, Family Business and SME Policy. Dr. Dwivedi has published his research in various leading journals. He is part of the India Team that leads the prestigious 'Global Entrepreneurship Monitor' research study. Also, he is co-author of GEM India Report 2014, 2015/16, 2016/17, 2017/18, 2018/19 and 2019/20. Dr. Dwivedi is trained in Application of Simulation for Entrepreneurship Teaching at the University of Tennessee, USA.

Acknowledgements

The GEM India Consortium is glad to probe the conditions that enable entrepreneurship to flourish or deteriorate, so that suitable interventions could be accordingly instituted. The consortium has been constantly putting in efforts to research the ways and means that could bolster the entrepreneurship scenario so that the entrepreneurs, the lifeblood of economies, continue to perform a potent role.

The GEM Report 2020–2021, throws light on entrepreneurial trends and practices amidst changing business and impact of COVID-19 on entrepreneurial activities in the country. We express gratitude to the Centre for Research in Entrepreneurship Education and Development (CREED), for providing financial support for this project.

- Our sincere thanks to the GEM Global Team at London Business School, Babson College and the GEM Data Team for their untiring support and direction.

- We would also like to heartily thank the national experts and the respondents of various surveys, for sparing their valuable time and sharing rich insights with us.

- We also express our gratitude to Ms. Simran Sodhi and Ms. Akansha Gupta, without their support, this task could not have been completed.

- The authors thank Ms. Julie Shah, Head-Department of Institutional Communication and Public Relations, for facilitating the publication of this report.

- We express our cordial thanks to the team members of Kantar, India for timely conducting and submitting data of APS.

Authors

Executive Summary

The GEM India 2020-21 report, explains the key aspects of entrepreneurship among Indians, by measuring their attitudes, activities and aspirations. The findings of the report, provide the policy-makers, a foundation for reviewing the current and prospective policies. The major findings and appropriate recommendations for policy-making are highlighted under the conclusion section of this report. The report uses a sample survey of 3,317 adults and national level experts. To ensure national representation, appropriate weights were used for age groups, gender and urban-rural categories.

KEY POINTS FROM THE ADULT POPULATION SURVEY (APS)

❑   Around 62% of the youth have reported that they know someone who has started a business recently.

❑   The results show that 82% of the population perceives that there is a good opportunity to start a business in their area. Of the 47 economies, India ranked 3rd for perceived opportunities.

❑   About 82% of the youth believe that they possess the skills and knowledge to start a business. The statistics have marginally decreased from last year.

❑   The data shows that fear of failure has increased by 1 percent among youth. It was 56% in 2019-20, whereas, it has increased to 57% for 2020-21. The data highlights that there is a fear of failure among youth to choose and to be entrepreneurs.

❑   The level of intentions among the population, keeps changing and compared to the last year's survey, a significant negative change has been observed. Entrepreneurial intentions had been 33.3% in 2019–20, which fell to 20.31% in 2020–21. This negative change of perception may be due to the lockdown and impact of the COVID 19 Pandemic.

❑   The rate of Total Early-stage Entrepreneurship Activity (TEA) in India has also been severely affected by the pandemic and it came down to 5.34% from last year's 15%. The finding is also in line with other economic parameters of the country. The change has been observed at 64 percent, decreased from 15 percent in 2019-20.

❑   The findings reveal that pandemic has negatively impacted Total Entrepreneurial Activities in the country. However, it is more severe in case of the female youth. Female entrepreneurial activities are decreased by 79 percent, while the male entrepreneurial activities are decreased by 53 percent.

❑   The observation for established business ownership is important and it is found that 5.88% of youth have reported that they are engaged in an established business. The numbers decreased by 51 percent from last year's 11.92%.

❑   An important finding of this survey is that 53 percent of Indians reported that they know someone who has started a new business and a slightly high proportion of 60 percent of the youth perceived that they know someone who stopped a business during the pandemic. It is also important to mention here that more than 84 percent of the youth in India, reported that the pandemic has delayed the business operations in the country.

❑   An effort has also been made to understand the impact of pandemics on household income. The results presented in the report, indicate that pandemic has a very negative impact on household income. In India, about 44 percent of youth have perceived that pandemic has harmed their household income.

KEY TAKES FROM NES 2020-21

❑   Out of the low-income economies (India, Angola, Burkina Faso, Togo and Morocco), India has been tremendously good as an entrepreneurial ecosystem. India is a leading ecosystem for entrepreneurs, as compared to the other low-income economies, across all pillars of framework conditions.

❏ Across a couple of the government-related framework conditions, India did better in 2020, than it did in 2019. This improvement in institutional support for entrepreneurship is reflected in the experts' assessment of the government's response to the pandemic, where, India's 6.6 score places it fifth among all GEM participating economies.

❏ Experts scored the entrepreneurial response at 7.0 (10th among all GEM participating economies). This reflects a reasonably strong estimation of how entrepreneurs weathered the challenges of 2020.

❏ *Entrepreneurial Finance:* The financial ecosystem for entrepreneurs is highly favourable in the country. Every year, the country is putting a lot of resources to strongly back the financial ecosystem of the country. In National Expert Survey, the experts gave India, a 6.4 score on 'Access to entrepreneurial finance', the highest amongst all GEM participating economies. This score is higher than the previous year's score (2019 score was 5.7).

❏ *Government Policy & Programme:* For 'Government policy: taxes and bureaucracy', experts scored the economy at 5.7 in 2020 (sixth among the GEM participating economies), up from 5.1 in 2019, while for 'Government entrepreneurship programs', India scored 5.8 in 2020 (11th among GEM participating economies), compared to 5.1 in 2019. Overall, government programmes are doing very well in providing a favourable ecosystem to entrepreneurs. Most importantly, there is an adequate count of government programmes, along with the support from business incubators and science parks.

❏ *Entrepreneurial Education:* India stands at rank 6th (Entrepreneurship Education in Schools) and 14th (Entrepreneurship Education in Post Schools), among other GEM participating Countries.

❏ *The Commercial and legal infrastructure* is improved in the country. As compared to the last year, this year, we can observe a considerable rise in the rank. The country has 6th rank now, which was 8th in 2020, globally.

❏ *Physical Infrastructure in India:* Out of all the framework conditions, this is one of the outperforming EFC, in the Indian entrepreneurial ecosystem. All dimensions of this condition are equally favourable for entrepreneurs. The current rank in this EFC is 16th, which was 29th, during the previous year.

❏ *Research and Development:* Research and development of the nation, create commercial opportunities for entrepreneurs. The overall strength of this framework condition is normally good. The current rank of this EFC is 3rd, which was 6th, during the previous year.

❏ *Social and Cultural Norms in India:* This framework condition is contributing very well, in making of the country's favourable ecosystem for entrepreneurs. There has been an improvement in the rank. The current rank of this EFC is 8th compared to 12th, during the previous year.

❏ The National Entrepreneurship Context Index (GEM NECI), provides policymakers with insights, on how to foster such an environment. The NECI summarises the assessment *of Entrepreneurship Framework Conditions into a single composite score of the ease of starting and developing a business. The index measures the 12 Entrepreneurial Environment Conditions (EFCs), which make up the context, in which entrepreneurial activity takes place in a country.*

❏ *In its latest ranking, Indonesia, Netherlands, Taiwan and India are the top four.*

Business and Entrepreneurship Perspective in India

1.1 INDIAN ECONOMY: AN OVERVIEW

India persists to be the 6th largest economy in the world with the GDP of 3049.70 billion dollars and the 3rd largest in context to PPP ranking with 10,207.29 billion dollars. The year 2020 has witnessed every economy at risk. All economies have suffered huge losses, which resulted in the contraction of economic figures. Believed to be a one-in-a-century global crisis, 90 percent of the countries are expected to have a contraction in their GDP. Indian economy also faced the crisis of coronavirus, but, eventually the steps taken by the Indian government helped the country in a V-shaped economic recovery. India implemented a timely lockdown, from mid-March to May. This helped in curbing the spread of coronavirus in the country. But this brought the Indian economy to a standstill, which affected in the contraction of GDP. This year the GDP of India contracted up to 23.9 percent. The complete lockdown for two months has affected the economy badly, though from June 2020 the economy experienced some recovery. The Government of India (GOI) has strategized the fiscal policy in such a way that funds would be available for all essential activities even if there is a sharp decline in revenue receipts.

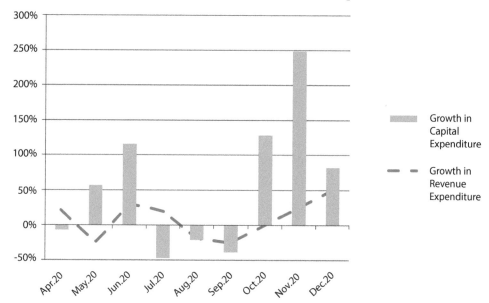

Figure 1.1 Trends of monthly expenditure and revenues of Central Government (2020-21)
Source: Economic Survey 2020-21

Considering the innovative aspect of India, this year the country has bagged 48th position in Global Innovation Index. For the first time, India has entered amongst the top 50 innovative countries in theworld. In the last five years, India has jumped 33 positions from 81st in 2005 to 48th in 2020 out of 131 countries. Considering Central and South Asia, India stands 1st as an innovative country and 3rd amongst lower-middle-income economies. India has also improved its position in innovation outputs from 69th in 2015 to 45th in 2020. In fact, the KTO ranking of India has halved to 27 in 2020 as compared to 49 in 2015. In creative output, it has improved to 64 in 2020 from 95 in 2015. Still, some areas need attention; i.e. education, tertiary inbound mobility, ICT access and use and ease of starting a business. India further needs improvement in strengthening institutions and business sophistication.

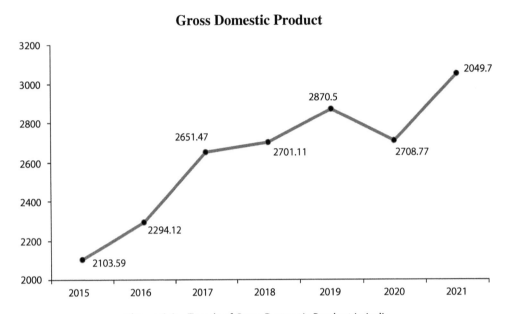

Figure 1.2   Trends of Gross Domestic Product in India

Source: *Statista. https://www.statista.com/statistics/263771/gross-domestic-product-gdp-in-india/*

Even at the time of pandemic crisis, the GOI was focused across all sectors that needed attention. Indian government has paid considerable attention on the bare necessities of its citizens. Major schemes for bare necessities in 2020 include: phase II of Swachh Bharat Mission, 109.2 lakh houses sanctioned on 18th January, 2021 under Pradhan Mantri Awaas Yojna (PMAY), Jal Jeevan Mission, Sahaj Bijli Har Ghar Yojana – Saubhagya.

Figure 1.3   Various Rankings of India

1.2 INITIATIVES BY GOVERNMENT TO SUPPORT ENTREPRENEURSHIP, INNOVATION AND STARTUPS

Being a challenging year; many MSMEs, businesses and startups have faced downfall and crisis. In these tough times, the GOI has been supportive and it provided various aids and remedies to people for compensating their losses. Following are some of the schemes that have supported businesses, startups and entrepreneurs.

Atmanirbhar Bharat

Under Atmanirbhar Bharat, the government announced many structural reforms in 2020-21. These reforms were related to agriculture, MSMEs, labour, business process outsourcing (BPO), power, PSUs, mineral sector. Some other reforms focused on strengthening of productive capacity. Such reforms included industry, space, defense, education, social infrastructure. Further, some reforms were focused towards ease of doing business, which includes financial market reforms, corporates and administration. Following table showcase the reforms which have supported the startups and entrepreneurs.

Table 1.1 Major reforms under Atmanirbhar Bharat scheme

MSMEs	❏ New definition of MSMEs
	❏ Removal of separation between manufacturing and service MSMEs
Ease of Doing Business	❏ Direct listing of securities
	❏ Reduced timeline for completion of rights issued by companies
	❏ Private companies listing NCDs not to be regarded as listed companies
	❏ Including provisions of Part IXA of Companies Act, 2013
	❏ Lower penalties for all defaults for small companies, one person companies, producer companies and start-ups
	❏ Simplified proforma for incorporating Company Electronically Plus

Source: *Economic Survey*

The most crucial reform has been the new definition of MSMEs. Through this modification, the MSMEs benefit the expansion and growth of entrepreneurs. Along with this, maximum MSMEs would be benefited from the government incentives, which would further help them in enhancing their production, getting collateral-free loans, market support and promotion in exports. The GOI has pooled hefty amount for Atmanirbhar Bharat to support MSMEs and others sectors.

Start-up Intellectual Property Protection

In 2020, the scheme is further extended to facilitate the IPR Protection among startups. Through this scheme, startups can seek assistance from the facilitators to file their application. Throughout the year, 2020 had the maximum number of applications filed by the startups with 1800 applications. This eased the procedure for the startups. As of June 2020, there were 510 patent facilitators and 392 trademark facilitators who have worked with startups and provided free-of-charge services to them.

Funds of Funds for Startups (FFS)

Under this initiative, funds were accumulated for the startups. SIDBI has contributed INR 4326.95 crores and more funds were generated from other sources. In this year, 4509.16 crores were invested in 384 startups in India.

Startup Yatra

This initiative is taken by the government to search for entrepreneurial talent. Day-long boot camps are conducted in Tier 2 and Tier 3 cities of India for entrepreneurial talent. Till date, the initiative has been implemented across 23 states and in 207 districts. This has impacted 78346 aspiring entrepreneurs.

CHAMPIONS

The Creation and Harmonious Application of Modern Process for Increasing the Output and National Strength (CHAMPIONS) was launched on 9th May 2020. It is an online platform to help MSMEs. This platform is a single window solution that caters to all needs of MSMEs. This helps in the growth of smaller units, as they can easily resolve their problems and can smoothly run their enterprise.

1.3 EASE OF DOING BUSINESS IN INDIA

Ease of doing business is a ranking system which is established by the World Bank Group annually. The ranking includes 190 economies which are examined on the basis of 12 areas of business regulations.

Table 1.2 Measurement areas in Ease of Doing Business

Opening a business	1. Starting a business
	2. Employing workers
Getting a location	3. Dealing with construction permits
	4. Getting electricity
	5. Registering property
Accessing finance	6. Getting credit
	7. Protecting minority investors
Dealing with day-to-day operations	8. Paying taxes
	9. Trading across borders
	10. Contracting with the government
Operating in a secure business environment	11. Enforcing contracts
	12. Resolving insolvency

Source: *Doing Business 2020*

In 2020, India stood at 63rd position out of 190 economies for Ease of Doing Business. Common features that are prevalent in top 20 economies includes: widespread use of electronic system, smooth online business incorporation process, online tax filling facilities, online property transfer, high degree of transparency and quality control index. This provides a roadmap to other economies on how to improve ease of doing business in their economies.

India is amongst the top 10 economies that have improved the most across three or more areas. This year, India has worked on starting a business, dealing with construction permits, trading across borders and resolving insolvency. India has taken a long jump for improving its position from 142nd in 2014 to 63rd in 2020. In addition to this, this is the consistently 3rd year when India has been in the top 10 improvers.

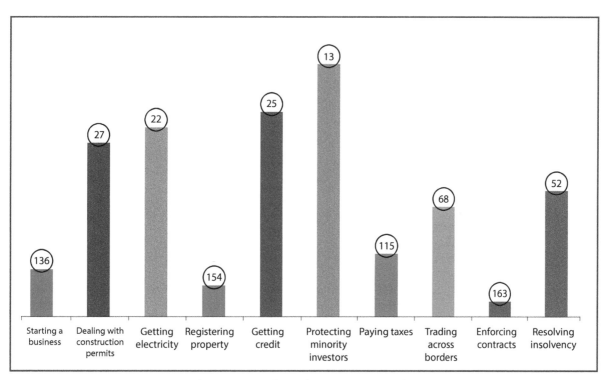

Figure 1.4 Ranking of Doing Business (India)

Source: *https://www.doingbusiness.org/en/data/exploreeconomies/india*

Some of the major reforms by India that helped in improving its positions are:

❏ The GOI has launched web based SPICe+ and AGILE-PRO-S form.

❏ Mumbai and Delhi has launched one-stop shop portal.

❏ Simplified the process of obtaining building permits and occupancy cum completion certificates.

❏ Reduced the number of days required for getting electricity connection.

❏ Smoother and easier trading across borders.

❏ Delhi and Mumbai has dedicated commercial courts for early redressal of commercial disputes.

1.4 START-UP ECOSYSTEM OF INDIA 2021

A healthy startup ecosystem is very crucial for the aspiring startups to set up their business. It is further required for the existing business for a sustainable existence and growth.

As per Startup Ecosystem Index 2021, India has improved its position by 3 spots and has entered among the top 20 countries. India stands at 20th position in the ranking. In the Global Startup Ecosystem Index of top cities, India has 3 cities; Bangalore at 10th spot, New Delhi at 14th and Mumbai at 16th position globally. This year, India has 43 cities in total that have been ranked, out of which 3 lie in top 20 positions with Bangalore among top 10. There are 9 new cities that have entered in this year's ranking. Out of all the cities, 3 cities are in top 100, 8 cities are in top 200 and 20 in top 500. Though, in 2020, India dropped by 6 spots. But, the country has taken many crucial steps and worked hard to maintain its position in top 20. Among the Asia-Pacific region, India ranked 5th in the startup ecosystem.

Table 1.3 Cities Ranking in Global Startup Ecosystem Index 2021

National Rank	City	Global Rank	Over-performing Industry
1.	Bangalore	10	Transportation
2.	New Delhi	14	Social & Leisure
3.	Mumbai	16	
4.	Pune	104	E-commerce & Retail
5.	Hyderabad	106	Education
6.	Chennai	133	Education
7.	Ahmedabad	176	
8.	Jaipur	195	Education

Source: Global Startup Ecosystem Index Report 2021

However, Indian ecosystem has some areas that need improvement. There are some issues that need attention regarding infrastructural problems; internet speed is slow when compared to other top countries, and frequent power outages. India needs to pay attention on the fact that startups cannot survive solely on local market. They need to find ways through which startups can access multiple markets.

The Index also discusses about the Industry Analysis and Ranking. In E-commerce & Retail Technology Ranking, India has two cities with New Delhi at 9th spot and Bangalore at 18th position. New Delhi has improved by 5 positions but, Bangalore has slipped by 8 spots. In the Education Technology ranking Bangalore improved its position by four and stands at 6th position whereas New Delhi improved by 1 spot and stands at 13th position. Next is the Fintech ranking, which consists of two cities Bangalore and Mumbai. Bangalore stands at 7th position and Mumbai at 10th. Both of them have improved their spot by 3 and 6 respectively. Foodtech ranking has New Delhi and Bangalore at spot 17 and 20 respectively. Both of them have slipped their spots. New Delhi slipped by 3 spots and Bangalore by 10. In the Marketing & Sales Technology ranking Bangalore has improved its position by 1 and stands at 9th position, however, New Delhi slipped by 11 spots and bagged 25th spot. The Social & Leisure Technology ranking has only one city as New Delhi at 7th spot. Performance of India has lowered in Software & Data as ranking of Bangalore slipped by 7 positions and stands at 17th spot. The Transportation ranking has improved as Bangalore stands at 4th and New Delhi at 7th position. India needs to improve in Energy & Environment Technology Ranking, Hardware & IoT Ranking and Health Technology Ranking. These lists do not include any Indian city.

Figure 1.5 List of Unicorns in India

Source: https://www.cnbctv18.com/startup/india-is-home-to-21-unicorns-collectively-valued-at-732-billion-hurun-global-unicorn-list-2020-6538511.htm

1.5 WORLD COMPETITIVENESS RANKING

India is home to 21 unicorns and 5 pantheons. It is currently the fourth-largest unicorn base in the world. As per estimates, by 2025, India will have 100 unicorns which will create approximately 1.1 million direct jobs. However, in 2021, two unicorns exit the market in India. The World Economic Forum came up with The Global Competitiveness Report Special Edition for the first time in 2020. It focuses on how countries are performing on the road to recovery from COVID-19 pandemic. Since the outbreak of pandemic, many developing and advanced economies faced the problem of unemployment. By the end of 2020, approximately 245 million full-time jobs are lost globally. This special edition aims to support the global economies in recovery strategies by discussing holistic approach and reform objectives. The report has tried to access the readiness among countries for achieving the future transformation across various areas. In this report, economies are scored out of 100 as per their performance on economic transformation priorities in the year 2020. Following table showcases the scores attained by India.

Table 1.4   Performance of India across various transformation priorities in 2020

S.No.	Transformation Priorities	Ranking
1.	Ensure public institutions embed strong governance principles and a long-term vision and build trust by serving their citizens	49.4
2.	Upgrade infrastructure to accelerate the energy transition and broaden access to electricity and ICT	72.6
3.	Shift to more progressive taxation, rethinking how corporations, wealth and labour are taxed, nationally and in an international cooperative framework	55.8
4.	Update education curricula and expand investment in the skills needed for jobs and "markets of tomorrow"	43.5
5.	Rethink labour laws and social protection for the new economy and the new needs of the workforce	44.4
6.	Increase incentives to direct financial resources towards long-term investments, strengthen stability and expand inclusion	54.5
7.	Rethink competition and anti-trust frameworks needed in the Fourth Industrial Revolution, ensuring market access, both locally and internationally	57.3
8.	Facilitate the creation of "markets of tomorrow", especially in areas that require public-private collaboration	40.2
9.	Incentivize and expand patient investments in research, innovation and invention that can create new "markets of tomorrow"	32.5
10.	Incentivize firms to embrace diversity, equity and inclusion to enhance creativity	45.1

Source: The Global Competitiveness Report, Special Edition 2020

1.6 STATES' STARTUP RANKING

States' Startup Ranking 2018 has been the first report that provided insights about state-driven initiatives. The first edition was a key learning which helped in identifying numerous practices across the country. Followed by this, States' Startup Ranking Report 2019 was the second edition. According to the second ranking, the states and UTs were divided into two categories – Category-X and Category-Y. All the states and UTs were evaluated on seven pillars, with 30 action points.

"Identifying good practices, augmenting mutual learning, building capacity of key stakeholders across the Indian startup landscape and propelling States to advance ecosystems with their jurisdictions" is the objective of States' Startup Ranking 2020. The States' Startup Ranking Framework 2020 is more robust and evolved. This year the framework has categorized the states and UTs on the basis of population. The categorization is done for the uniformity in the evaluation process. Some more reforms are done by changing the pillars of framework.

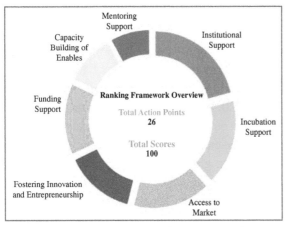

Figure 1.6 States' Startup Ranking Framework 2020	Figure 1.7 States' Startup Ranking Framework 2019
Source: Startup India	*Source: Startup India*

This framework includes seven pillars: Institutional Support, Fostering Innovation & Entrepreneurship, Access to Market, Incubation Support, Funding Support, Mentorship Support and Capacity Building of Enablers. The framework 2020 has 26 Action Points as compared to 30 Action Points in Ranking Framework 2019. Fig. 5 and Fig. 6 provide a comparison between Framework of 2020 Ranking and 2019 Ranking of States' Startup.

1.7 IMPACT OF COVID – 19 ON BUSINESSES

Every economy and every sector has been hit due to COVID crisis across the globe. MSMEs are the one which have been affected the most due to nation-wide lockdown. This is the sector which has a considerable share in GDP and employ nearly 11 crore people in India. Globally, the entrepreneurs have been affected by the pandemic. According to a global report, most of the entrepreneurs have been worried about sustainability of their business. According to these entrepreneurs, trading was reduced, which was the biggest challenge for them. Other challenges were like; delay in payments and problem in paying their upkeep of business, because of which they also had to lay off their staff. Across the world, 61 percent entrepreneurs were threatened about the existence of their business. Similarly, in India, 60 percent entrepreneurs believed that their business is under threat. Globally, 74.9 percent has reported loss in trading. Although there are a few entrepreneurs (26 percent) who faced no problems in business. In India, 81 percent people had to bear losses in trade and because of this, 39 percent of businesses had to lay off their staff. Some entrepreneurs also shared that due to closure of schools they had to pay lot of care towards their kids which restricted their working hours. This restriction has created problems in running their business smoothly. In India, 3 percent entrepreneurs could not work due to pandemic; 21 percent started working mostly from their home; 42 percent reported that they have completely started working from home; 15 percent were already operating their business from home and 19 percent entrepreneurs were still working from their business premise.

Nearly 68.2 percent entrepreneurs globally changed their business plans due to pandemic and 39.4 percent entrepreneurs encountered new business opportunities. In India, nearly 70 percent entrepreneurs changed their business plans and developed alternative plans for their business and approximately 45 percent entrepreneurs in India explored new business opportunities. Majorly, the entrepreneurs have discussed five parameters of new business opportunities in the pandemic; i.e. digitalization, health & well-being, shift from global to local, sustainability and inclusion and new business model & repositioning of the business.

In India, 22.5 percent entrepreneurs expanded into online trading at the time of pandemic. To sustain their businesses, nearly 25 percent of Indian entrepreneurs have applied for government support. Globally, approximately half of the entrepreneurs were optimistic about their business survival and 52 percent entrepreneurs focused on short term planning.

There are few entrepreneurs who believed to have higher growth in business during pandemic and due to this they have added more employees. Over 70 percent entrepreneurs globally believe that they will have to increase the count of employees beyond pandemic. Approximately 45 percent of Indian entrepreneurs believe that there would be positive impact on their business in the long run. The parameters which are believed to be the nature of positive long term impact are: business acceleration, business efficiency and resilience, business refocus and business opportunities. SMEs in India also believe that due to pandemic businesses focused on sustainable growth, reduced costs and more access to worldwide markets, which has resulted in improved processes and practices.

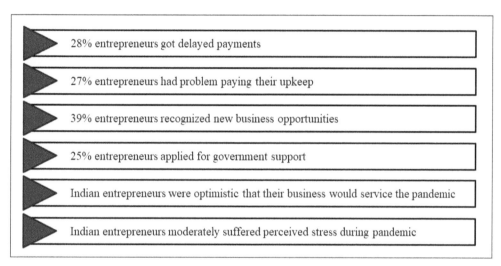

Figure 1.8   Indian Entrepreneurs during pandemic
Source: *Entrepreneurship during the Covid-19 Pandemic, King's College London*

1.8 WOMEN ENTREPRENEURSHIP

Out of 58.5 million entrepreneurs in India, 8.05 million entrepreneurs are women, which count as 14% of total entrepreneurs in India. Further, out of these 8.05 million women entrepreneurs, 79% businesses are self-financed and small sized. However, these counts of women entrepreneurs are not very encouraging. The contribution of Indian women entrepreneurs is very low (17%) as compared to the global average which stands at 39%. Though, Government of India is putting considerable efforts to improve these figures. Many initiatives and schemes have been introduced to encourage women towards entrepreneurship. The GOI has started a concentrated platform for women entrepreneurship (WEP) that would provide an ecosystem for aspiring as well as existing women entrepreneurs. The platform has three pillars:

Iccha Shakti - helps the aspiring women entrepreneurs in starting their enterprise.
Gyaan Shakti – helps in providing the suited knowledge and ecosystem to support women entrepreneurship.
Karma Shakti – helps in providing hands-on support for starting and scaling their business.

Under Stand-Up India scheme, the GOI provides many incentives for women entrepreneurs like financial support with the aim of at least one women entrepreneur per bank branch. India needs to improve the position of women entrepreneurs, still we have some names which are very successful as a women entrepreneur in India.

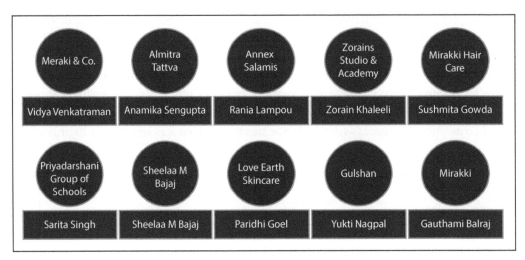

Figure 1.9 Top 10 women entrepreneurs in India

Source: *https://www.fortuneindia.com/enterprise/top-10-women-entrepreneurs-in-2020-21-by-the-indian-alert/10549*

Global Entrepreneurship Monitor (GEM) Conceptual Framework

2

OVERVIEW

The Global Entrepreneurship Monitor (GEM) is the world's largest study of entrepreneurs and entrepreneurial perceptions. The GEM report 2020-21 is a part of the 22nd survey of the global report, which provides the result on 46 countries. The report provides data on two important parameters: entrepreneurial attributes and activities, and the entrepreneurial ecosystem. There are data on entrepreneurial attributes and activities of 43 economies and the entrepreneurial ecosystem of 45 economies. The 22nd global report represents the sustained research efforts of 46 different national teams, each collecting data in a manner that is consistent and coherent, allowing comparisons between different economies for the same year, and for the same economy in different years. The present report has carefully assessed the impact of the COVID-19 pandemic on levels of entrepreneurial activity around the world and on attitudes and perceptions.

Ensuring the entrepreneurship development process is important to all economies, particularly at the time of a pandemic. While many new businesses have been deferred or disrupted by the pandemic, others have been able to grab new opportunities, ranging across the economic spectrum from the production of pharmaceuticals to the online purchase of takeaway food. This Global Report presents the first evidence-based worldwide assessment of the competing balance between those challenges and opportunities.

The Global Entrepreneurship Monitor (GEM) project started in 1997 as a collaborative initiative by Michael Hay of London Business School (LBS) and Bill Bygrave of Babson College, USA. The survey was intended for collection and analysis of harmonized data on the prevalence of nascent entrepreneurship and young enterprises across nations. It aimed at generating and propagating knowledge on entrepreneurship in the world by exploring entrepreneurial behaviour and attitude of individuals and the national context, and its effect on entrepreneurship. The Global Report 2020-21 includes more than 130,000 individual APS interviews, which means that, up to the present, a total of more than 3.2 million adults in more than 120 different economies have participated in the APS since the first survey of 10 countries in 1999.

The GEM global report 2020-21 has provided a holistic understanding regarding participating economies, regions and income levels. The 46 economies in this latest survey belong to four different regions and three different economic classifications as defined by the World Bank. The Middle East and Africa region includes 12 economies, while the Central and East Asia region has six economies, across all income groups. Latin America and the Caribbean include eight economies from the middle-and high-income groups. The Europe and North America region has 20 economies, but is least diverse in terms of income group, with just one economy in the middle-income group and the rest categorized as high-income (Please see Table 2.1).

Table 2.1 Classification of economies participating in the GEM Survey 2020-21

	Low-Income	Middle-Income	High-Income
Central & East Asia	India	Kazakhstan, Indonesia	Japan, Republic of Korea, Taiwan
Europe and North America		Russian Federation	Austria, Canada, Croatia, Cyprus, Germany, Greece, Italy, Latvia, Luxembourg, Netherlands, Norway, Poland, Slovak Republic, Slovenia, Spain, Sweden, Switzerland, United Kingdom, United States
Latin America and Caribbean		Brazil, Colombia, Guatemala, Mexico	Chile, Panamá, Puerto Rico, Uruguay
Middle East and Africa	Angola, Burkina Faso, Egypt, Morocco, Togo	Iran	Israel, Kuwait, Oman, Qatar, Saudi Arabia, United Arab Emirates

Source: GEM Global Report 2020-21

2.1 THE GEM CONCEPTUAL FRAMEWORK

The GEM is the largest ongoing study of entrepreneurial dynamics in the world. The main objective of the GEM is to provide data on entrepreneurship that will be utilized for making meaningful comparisons, both within the nation as well as around the world. To achieve this objective, the GEM collects data annually from two main sources i.e., adult population survey (APS) and national experts survey (NES). The APS provides information regarding the level of entrepreneurial activity in the country whereas the NES gives insights into the entrepreneurial start-up environment in each economy/country concerning the nine entrepreneurial framework conditions.

As per GEM norms, a minimum of 2000 randomly selected adults (18 - 64 years old) must be surveyed in each country. The APS is conducted every year, from April to June, by independent survey vendors, using the GEM questionnaire (Appendix II contains a list of countries surveyed, as well as the information about the sample size). The APS is conducted via a mix of face-to-face or telephonic interviews. The survey tries to find out whether the youth of the country is involved in starting or running a new or established business, and about individual attitudes and perceptions of entrepreneurship, along with demographic details such as age, gender and education. The APS data provides understanding about individual decision to start or continue a business, and the entrepreneurial journey from intentions through to business conception, business set up, and subsequent growth and development.

The NES is conducted every year, during the same period, by the GEM national teams comprised of at least 36 experts (four experts from each of the nine components of the entrepreneurial conditions framework), using the GEM questionnaire. The NES focuses on the entrepreneurial context that influences an individual decision to start a new business, and subsequent decisions to sustain and grow that business. It provides an in-depth understanding of the substantial impact of the environment on the entrepreneurship development process. The GEM research assesses the national entrepreneurship environment through expert evaluation of nine Entrepreneurial Framework Conditions (EFCs). They range from the ease of access to finance to social support for entrepreneurship, and from the adequacy of entrepreneurial education to the availability and cost of essential business services. For this cycle, the GEM research included new questions on how adequately entrepreneurs in general — and governments in particular — have responded to the economic challenges and opportunities of the pandemic.

Both the APS and the NES provide a comprehensive understanding of entrepreneurship in each participating economy. The GEM Conceptual Framework is set out in Figure 2.1 and depicts the relationship between entrepreneurship and its regional and national environment. The level of entrepreneurial activity of a country is the result of its population's assessment of entrepreneurial opportunities and their entrepreneurial potential (i.e. motivation and capacity). Recognition of opportunities and entrepreneurial potential is influenced by both specific entrepreneurial framework conditions and general national framework conditions. While entrepreneurial framework conditions are also influenced by the general framework conditions within a nation, both of these are shaped by social, cultural, political and economic factors. The National framework conditions reflect the phases of economic development (low-income, middle-income and high-income).

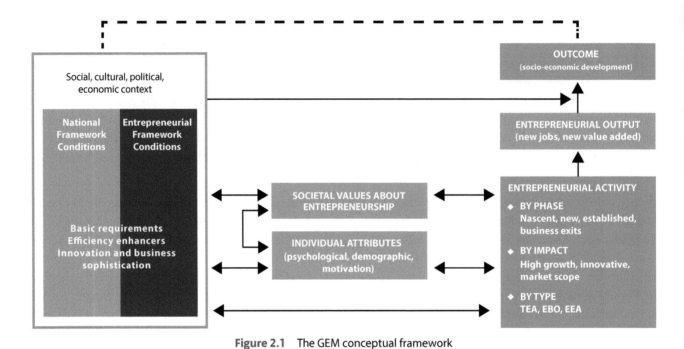

Figure 2.1 The GEM conceptual framework
Source: *GEM Global Report 2020-21*

2.2 ENTREPRENEURIAL FRAMEWORK CONDITIONS

Entrepreneurship is not merely an intrinsic pursuit of entrepreneurs in isolation of the society to which they belong. An economy's entrepreneurial activity depends on various factors: the availability of capital; the concentration on building up entrepreneurial skills in educational programmes; the general thrust of national bankruptcy laws; the administrative burdens imposed on new enterprises by the state; and the capability of the research environment for converting new inventions into saleable products. Therefore, to address these issues, the GEM conceptual model also tries to understand the entrepreneurial framework conditions of the country. From Figure 2.2, it is clear that the entrepreneurial framework conditions of an economy are one of the important variables of the GEM conceptual model. The nine components identified by the global consortium of experts and used consistently for assessing the entrepreneurial framework conditions of nations are as follows.

❑ **Finance:** The availability of financial resources, equity debt for SMEs (including grants and subsidies) and the extent to which taxes or regulations are either size-neutral or encourage SMEs

❑ **Government policies:** The presence and quality of direct programmes to assist new and growing firms at all levels of government (national, regional and municipal)

❑ **Entrepreneurial education and training:** The extent to which training in creating or managing SMEs is incorporated within the education and training system at all levels (primary, secondary and post-school)

- ❑ **R&D transfer:** The extent to which national research and development will lead to new commercial opportunities and is available to SMEs

- ❑ **Commercial and legal infrastructure:** The presence of property rights and commercial, accounting, and other legal services and institutions that support or promote SMEs

- ❑ **Entry regulation:** It contains two components: (i) Market dynamics: the level of change in markets from year to year, and (ii) Market openness: the extent to which new firms are free to enter the existing markets.

- ❑ **Physical infrastructure and services:** Ease of access to physical resources i.e., communication, utilities, transportation, land or space at a price that does not discriminate against SMEs

- ❑ **Cultural and social norms:** The extent to which social and cultural norms encourage or allow actions leading to new business methods or activities that can potentially increase personal wealth and income

- ❑ **Senior entrepreneurship:** The availability of policy interventions and social benefits for encouraging senior entrepreneurship.

2.3 SOCIAL VALUES TOWARDS ENTREPRENEURSHIP

The values and culture of society towards entrepreneurship facilitate the process of continuous supply of entrepreneurs in the society. Hence, to explore the relationship between social values and entrepreneurship, the GEM research also includes 'social value towards entrepreneurship' as one of the key variables. In this context, the GEM has been trying to understand how the society values entrepreneurship as a good career choice; if entrepreneurs have a high social status; and how media attention to entrepreneurship is contributing (or not) to the development of national entrepreneurial culture.

2.4 INDIVIDUAL ATTRIBUTES

The GEM model measures several individual attributes, i.e. perception of opportunities, perception of own capabilities to act entrepreneurially, fear of failure, and entrepreneurial intentions. These individual factors facilitate entrepreneurship activities. Apart from these individual-level factors, the GEM model also includes several demographic factors (gender, age, geographic location), and motivational aspects of starting new ventures.

2.5 ENTREPRENEURIAL ACTIVITY

Entrepreneurial activities are defined in terms of enterprise life-cycle approach (nascent, new venture, established venture, discontinuation), the types of activity (high growth, innovation, internationalization) and the sector of the activity (total early-stage entrepreneurial activity—TEA, social entrepreneurial activity—SEA, employee entrepreneurial activity—EEA). It also provides insights on ambitious entrepreneurial activity (both from the standpoint of an owner-managed venture and of an entrepreneurial employee).

The GEM's total entrepreneurial activity (TEA) includes the youths involved in the process of setting up new businesses as well as those who own and manage running businesses for up to 3.5 years. Hence, it collects data on entrepreneurial attitudes, activity, and aspirations in various phases of entrepreneurship; from general intentions through early-stage entrepreneurial activity to the status as established firms. The primary measure of entrepreneurship used by the GEM is the total early-stage entrepreneurial.

2.6 THE ENTREPRENEURSHIP PROCESS AND GEM OPERATIONAL DEFINITIONS

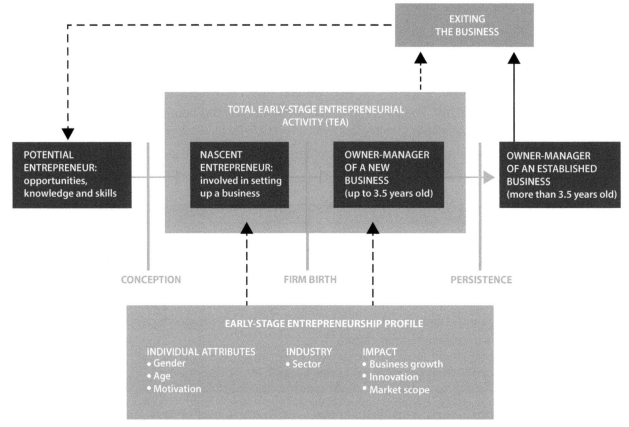

Figure 2.2 The Entrepreneurship Process and GEM Operational Definitions

There are several definitions of enterprise and entrepreneurship. But, given the objective of measuring entrepreneurial activity across space and time, the GEM has defined entrepreneurship as the activity of someone who is actively engaged in starting or running a new business. Identifying opportunities for a new business, thinking about starting a venture or having the intention to start a firm can be linked to entrepreneurship. However, according to the GEM's conceptualization, only active behaviour counts as entrepreneurship.

Entrepreneurship is not a unidimensional concept, rather it is a dynamic process and it has several interdependent dimensions. Hence, to have a holistic understanding of the concept; the GEM collects information across several phases of entrepreneurship (Figure 2.2) Total Entrepreneurial Activity (TEA) index, indicated by the shaded area in Figure 2.2. The TEA indicates the prevalence of business start-ups (or nascent entrepreneurs) and new firms in the adult (18 to 64 years of age) population— in other words, it captures the level of dynamic entrepreneurial activity in a country.

2.7 GEM OPERATIONAL DEFINITIONS OF MAJOR VARIABLES

❑ **Total early-stage entrepreneurial activity (TEA):** Percentage of individuals aged 18–64 who are either nascent entrepreneurs or owner-manager of a new business.

❑ **Nascent entrepreneurship rate:** Percentage of individuals aged 18–64 who are currently a nascent entrepreneur, i.e. actively involved in setting up a business they will own or co-own; this business has not paid salaries, wages, or any other payments to the owners for more than three months.

- ❑ **New business ownership rate:** Percentage of individuals aged 18–64 who are currently an owner/manager of a new business, i.e. owning and managing a running business that has paid salaries, wages, or any other payments to the owners for more than three months, but not more than 42 months.
- ❑ **Established business ownership rate:** Percentage of individuals aged 18–64 who are currently an owner-manager of an established business, i.e. owning and managing a running business that has paid salaries, wages, or any other payments to the owners for more than 42 months.
- ❑ **Business discontinuation rate:** Percentage of individuals aged 18–64 who in the past 12 months have discontinued a business, either by selling, shutting down, or otherwise discontinuing an owner/management relationship with the business. It may be noted that it is NOT a measure of business failure rates.

2.8 INDIVIDUAL ATTRIBUTES OF A POTENTIAL ENTREPRENEUR

- ❑ **Perceived opportunities:** Percentage of adults aged 18–64 involved in any stage of entrepreneurial activity excluded those who see good opportunities to start a business in the area where they live.
- ❑ **Perceived capabilities:** Percentage of adults aged 18–64 involved in any stage of entrepreneurial activity excluded those who believe they have the required skills and knowledge to start a business.
- ❑ **Entrepreneurial intentions:** Percentage of adults aged 18–64 involved in any stage of entrepreneurial activity excluded those who are latent entrepreneurs and intend to start a business within three years.
- ❑ **Fear of failure rate:** Percentage of adults aged 18–64 involved in any stage of entrepreneurial activity excluded those who report that fear of failure would prevent them from setting up a business.

2.9 THE GEM METHODOLOGY

The GEM is the largest ongoing empirical study of entrepreneurial dynamics in the world. The main objective of the GEM is to provide data on entrepreneurship that will be utilized for making meaningful comparisons, both within the nation as well as around the world. However, the specific objectives of the GEM survey are as follows:

- ❑ Do the level and types of entrepreneurial activity vary between economies, and, if so, to what extent?
- ❑ Does the level of entrepreneurial activity affect the country's rate of economic growth and prosperity?
- ❑ What factors make a country entrepreneurial?
- ❑ To provide a better insight into the process of formulation of effective and targeted policies aimed at stimulating entrepreneurship.

To address these questions, the GEM collects data annually from two main sources, namely (i) adult population survey (APS) and (ii) national experts survey (NES). The APS provides information regarding the level of entrepreneurial activity in the country whereas the NES gives insights into the entrepreneurship environment and culture in each participating country with regard to the nine entrepreneurial framework conditions.

2.10 ENTREPRENEURSHIP IN THE AGE OF COVID-19

Keeping the impact of COVID-19 in mind the GEM has included new questions regarding barriers and opportunities related to the pandemic as well as about the effects of the pandemic on household income. In the 2020-21 cycle, the APS enquired about the impacts of the pandemic in terms of its effects on the ease (or difficulty) of starting a venture, whether a new or existing business had to be curtailed, how growth expectations were affected, and about the adequacy (or otherwise) of government responses to the pandemic's economic impact. In the present report, an effort was made to understand the impact of the pandemic on key parameters of entrepreneurship in India.

2.11 ADULT POPULATION SURVEY (APS) IN INDIA

To assess the level of entrepreneurial activity in the country, primary data collection was done. A stratified random sampling method was used to select cities or villages across the country. Further, a city or village was divided into 4–5 strata and selection of a certain number of surveys starting points within each city/village was ensured. Moreover, with the help of The Kish Grid method households and adults were identified for the survey. Rather than selecting the respondents directly from the population, the two-stage sampling method was used. Hence, after identification of the household, the eligible age group was listed in descending order by age and an eligible respondent was identified by next birthday methods. If a selected person was not available at that time of the initial visit, at least 3 more visits were to be made before moving to another household in case of face-to-face interview, whereas 5 call-backs were done for telephonic interview.

In all, 3317 respondents aged between 18 and 64 years were included in the survey. More than 21 per cent of data were collected from each of four regions of India to ensure overall regional representation in the research (Table 2.2).

Table 2.2 Regional Distribution

	Number	Percentage
East	918	27.7
North	914	27.6
South	782	23.6
West	702	21.2
Total	3317	100.0

Apart from regional representation, an effort was also made to ensure appropriate representation of gender and location, i.e. male/female and urban/rural, respectively. For this purpose, appropriate weights were decided on the basis of various criteria (See Table 2.3 and 2.4).

Table 2.3 Rural/Urban Distribution

Location	Unweighted Sample	Percentage	Weighted sample	Percentage
Urban	2234	67.4	1112	33.5
Rural	1083	32.6	2205	66.5
Total	3317	100.0	3317	100.0

Table 2.4 Gender Distribution

Location	Unweighted Sample	Percentage	Weighted sample	Percentage
Male	1772	53.4	1697	51.2
Female	1545	46.6	1620	48.8
Total	3317	100.0	2217	100.0

The census data of 2011 were used for calculating the weights for various indices, i.e. male, female, urban, and rural. While the computation of the TEA index is the major outcome of this part of the study, it has also led to the identification of several characteristics of entrepreneurial individuals and firms. However, the GEM India Report 2020-21 is mainly a description of the level and nature of entrepreneurial activity among the adult population of the country and the quality of entrepreneurial framework conditions in the country.

The APS data is used to estimate the level of participation in entrepreneurial activity as well as to gather information on attitudes towards entrepreneurship and other related entrepreneurial activities in the country.

The second source of the GEM data is the NES, which conducts phone, email, or in-person interviews on the state of entrepreneurship in the country with 81 national experts from the public and private sectors. The interview was conducted with the help of a standardized questionnaire provided under the global GEM project. These local experts were selected for their expertise based on the "entrepreneurial framework conditions", such as government policy or research and development. The experts are equipped with rich perspectives not only about their respective professions but also in entrepreneurial knowledge. The questionnaire presented a series of statements reflecting the GEM perspective on conditions supporting entrepreneurship. The experts were asked to estimate the degree to which each factor was applicable for India. The final section solicits open-ended responses, which are coded into nine categories.

In all, 150 national experts were identified, approached, and requested for data collection and their consent was sought. Data was collected using e-mails and telephonic interviews. From 90 completed responses in all respects that were obtained, 81 were chosen for submission to the GEM, as against a requirement of 36. The average age of experts was 50.25 years and the average work experience was 20.79 years. The specialization of the experts is given in Table 2.5.

Table 2.5 Experts, Specialization (Table contains multiple responses)

S. No.	Specialisation	No.	Percentage
1	Entrepreneur	47	58.0
2	Investor, Financer, Banker	25	30.9
3	Policy Maker	23	28.4
4	Business and Support Services Provider	46	56.8
5	Educator, Teacher, Entrepreneurship Researcher	17	21.0

The data presented in Table 2.6 indicates that most experts qualify PhD and university level education. Some are from vocational, professional backgrounds. It is important to mention here that the experts who are researching the field of entrepreneurship are also included in this survey.

Table 2.6 Educational Qualification of Experts

SN	Educational Qualification	Number	Percentage
1	Secondary Education	4	5.0
2	Vocational professional	9	11.3
3	University/college	38	47.5
4	MA, Ph.D.	29	36.3
5	Total	80	100.0

The experts in the NES survey are classified into the male and female categories as well. To ensure female representation in the survey about 25 percent of the experts are selected from the female category whereas, the remaining 75 percent of the experts are male (See Table no 2.7).

Table 2.7 Gender of Experts

Gender	Frequency	Percent
Female	20	24.7
Male	61	75.3
Total	81	100.0

Measuring Entrepreneurship Activity in India

3

OVERVIEW

This chapter highlights the yearly trends and current situation through data points obtained from the survey of adults in the country. This **Adult Population Survey** (APS) identifies the entrepreneurial potential and confidence of the population over the entrepreneurial initiative by the government and individuals themselves. The APS is conducted by all the national teams involved in the years' reporting and survey of adults in their respective countries. Over 50 countries participate in the APS every year and more than 2000 adults on an average are surveyed. The survey is conducted with adults, entrepreneurs, students, nascent entrepreneurs, intended entrepreneurs, and others.

In the below table 3.1 (GEM India Snapshot), an overview of changes can be seen between two different years of 2019-20 to 2020-2021. The major highlights of the data in the GEM survey include; perceived opportunities, skills and knowledge of entrepreneurs, motivation, entrepreneurial intentions, and entrepreneurial activity in India. This chapter also provides a comparative analysis of the data with regional economies and regional analysis within the country as well. The regional aspect along with the gender aspect, are also discussed in this chapter. The proportion of entrepreneurial activity in India through various ways can also be seen in this chapter. Discussions for other data points like **Total Entrepreneurial Activity** (TEA) in India and its comparison with BRICS, Asia, and Pacific countries are also part of the analysis.

This chapter explains the TEA in the country. It also describes male-female comparison, comparison of age groups and TEA, and TEA comparison amongst various regions within India. The chapter also discusses job creation expectations, innovation, and motivations. Industry distribution is another crucial aspect of this attitudinal data. The data further highlights the entrepreneurial motivation and its value amongst youth and entrepreneurs.

Table 3.1   GEM India snapshot

Attitudes and Perceptions	Value (%)	Rank/43
Perceived opportunity	82.5	3
Perceived capability	81.7	5
Fear of failure	56.8	1
Entrepreneurial Intention	20.3	23
Easy to start a business	78.5	5

Entrepreneurial Activity	Value (%)	Rank
TEA 2020-21	5.3	39/43
TEA 2019-20	15.0	13/50
TEA 2018-19	11.4	22/48
The established business ownership rate	5.9	28/43
Entrepreneurial Employee Activity-EEA	0.1	43/43

Gender Equity	Value (%)
Male TEA	7.9
Female TEA	2.6

Motivation	% of TEA	Rank/50	% Female TEA	% Male TEA
Make a difference in the world	80.7	1	74.3	82.7
Build great wealth	74.7	12	71.2	75.8
Continue family tradition	76.8	1	75.5	77.2
Earn living because jobs are scarce	87.3	5	92.0	85.9

Source: *GEM Global report 2020-21*

3.1 ATTITUDES AND PERCEPTION

Individual perceptions reflect the intentions towards a certain goal. In the GEM terminology, it reflects the intent towards business opportunities for starting a business. The data in table 3.2 shows that about 62 percent of the youth have reported that they know someone who has recently started a new business which reflects that the majority of population is aware that someone they know is starting a new business. This helps them widen their understanding and know the importance of starting a new businesses in the country.

Table 3.2   Attitudes and perception to start a business in India

Attitudes and Perceptions	Value %	GEM Rank/43
Know someone who has started a new business	61.9	17
Good opportunities to start a business in my area	82.5	3
It is easy to start a business	78.5	5
Personally have the skills and Knowledge	81.7	5
Fear of failure (opportunity)	56.8	1
Entrepreneurial intentions	20.3	23

Source: *GEM India Survey 2020-21*

The majority of the country's population (over 82 percent), perceives that there are good business opportunities in the area they live. While this reflects the notion of the population, the intention to take these opportunities has been seen as one-fourth of the same percentage. This shows the positive intentions of adults towards entrepreneurship.

Amongst the surveyed individuals, more than 78 percent perceive that it is easy to start a business in India. Perceived intentions lead to actions in the coming time. This percentage has greatly increased, mainly due to the vigorous efforts by the government and new policy formulations. This easy-to-start business greatly depends upon the efforts of the government towards ease of doing business and start-up. The percentage for opportunities available and ease to start a business are almost the same. This highlights that individuals are highly positive about starting a new business venture.

Another important data point in this survey is the skill and knowledge amongst the surveyed individuals. The data shows that nearly 82 percent of the population is confident that they possess the required skills and knowledge to start a new business. This data is reflected in the previous data points as well, however, the same is not contemplated in the fear of failure amongst these individuals. This data table shows that nearly 57 percent of the population is afraid of starting a new business due to many known and unknown reasons. Fear of failure is an important perception and keeps individuals away from starting their new business even when the person possesses all the resources, has great skills, the external environment is supportive. It is somehow attached in the mindset and it needs great effort to overcome the fear of failure and also leads to early failure, if the same individual starts a new business. Fear of failure is very relevant to the middle and lower-income classes of society. As entrepreneurship is a task of risk and uncertainty, this statement helps us understand this particular trait amongst Indians. Fear of failure is inflicted on individuals either naturally or due to social perceptions regarding business.

The entrepreneurship intention data in this table reflects a clear downward trend and provides important evidence for the effect of the pandemic in the country. The entrepreneurship intentions for surveyed individuals is at 20 percent and ranks 23rd amongst 43 countries surveyed. This reflects that entrepreneurial intentions are getting affected by the ongoing pandemic situation and it is reflected in the fear of failure amongst the surveyed individuals. Researchers perceive that existence of a good opportunity and having the required skills to act upon that, do not necessarily lead to start-up intentions. An idea or an opportunity may trigger in anybody's mind who can think, but ideation and having start-up intentions is a different part of it. In this scenario, the overall intention amongst individuals has gone down, creating a loop effect over the fear of failure as well.

Male-female attitudes and perceptions

In the below figure, a male-female data comparison is provided. The data depicts that both male and female respondents are equally progressing. However, amongst the four-variable fear of failure can be seen higher in females than males and it is reverse in other variables. In all other variables, males are leading by only a small margin while in fear of failure women are seen more fearful to start a new business.

In the data, we notice that males are leading in the percentage for the perceived opportunity (over 42 percent of males and 40 percent of females).

Another important data point is the knowledge and skills required to start a new business amongst males and females. The data shows that 42 percent of males and 38 percent of females perceive they possess the required skills to start a new business in India. The variation in data points highlights the role of perceptions in human intentions.

The data points for another important variable 'fear of failure', are interesting to understand, i.e. 47 percent of male fear to start a business due to chances of failure compared to the 50 percent by females. Change of attitude is important, as best entrepreneurs are an outcome of failures. An important generalization from this figure is that both males and females perceive high opportunity, skill and ease to start a business but a higher percentage believes that they will fail in their attempt. So, there is a need to create an environment where failure is not seen as a stigma and particularly in entrepreneurship it is used and understood as a fruitful exercise.

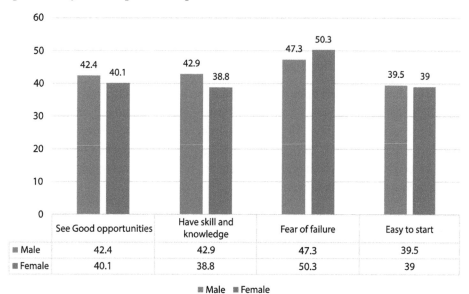

	See Good opportunities	Have skill and knowledge	Fear of failure	Easy to start
■ Male	42.4	42.9	47.3	39.5
■ Female	40.1	38.8	50.3	39

■ Male ■ Female

Figure 3.1   Attitudes and perception of males and females in India
Source: GEM India 2020-21

Comparison of attitudes and perception amongst East Asia and Pacific countries

In the below figure, data for the comparison of East Asia and Central Asian countries is given. It compares India, Kazakhstan, Indonesia, Taiwan and the Republic of Korea. The perception is measured in numbers and data reflects the gap in the perception of individuals' surveyed in these countries. Amongst the five countries represented in the table, India shows a high percentage to be perceiving good opportunities. However, the data also reflects that fear of failure is higher than the other countries. The existence of fear of failure keeps the country's population away from grabbing new opportunities in the entrepreneurship field. The data points for Indonesia are also very high and satisfactory. However, the fear of failure is not so high amongst Indonesians towards starting a new business. India leads with 81 percent of the population perceiving that they possess the knowledge to start a business in their country followed by Indonesia where 79 percent of respondents believe they possess enough knowledge to start a business. Indonesia is followed by Kazakhstan (64) and the Republic of Korea (55) and Taiwan (45). The data also reveals that more than 57 percent of Indians believe they have a fear of failure to start a business in the country compared to only 13 percent of individuals from the republic of Korea. This is an important statistic to analyze here that the smaller economies are more confident and perceive low fear of failure for business creation. More than 44 percent of Korean respondents believe they find an opportunity in their country and also 53 percent of Koreans believe they have the skill to start a business in their country.

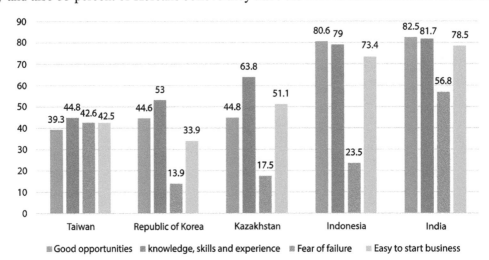

Figure 3.2   Attitudes and perception: A comparison of Central and East Asia
Source: *GEM Global Report 2020-21*

Region-wise perceptions and attitudes

Every year a region-wise data analysis is done to understand the data points from all four regions of the country. The data points highlight that samples must be collected from all the parts and regions of the country to highlight the country's regional perspective. Almost 82 percent of India's population perceives an opportunity to start a business. The data shows that more than 26 percent of East India are confident of opportunities in their area, 19 percent from North, 18 percent from South and 19 percent from West, perceive there are good opportunities in their area. The figure below highlights the data points.

There are visible regional differences amongst these variables and it can be seen that respondents from East India are more inclined to be entrepreneurs in the country. Perceived capabilities are higher in East India, followed by West and then North India. The data also shows that fear of failure is highest amongst East India and followed by North, South and least found in West part of the country. The major reason is that because the people perceive fewer opportunities, there is no fear of failure, as they will not even attempt. People in East India believe that it is easy to start a new business in their region followed by people in North, West, and South. The figure highlights the regional difference and the impact of the ongoing pandemic on the population.

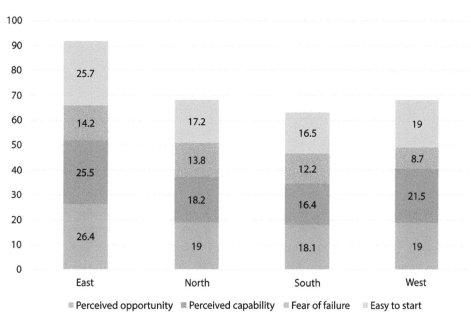

Figure 3.3 Perception and Attitudes: A comparison of the Indian region
Source: GEM India Survey 2020-21

3.2 ENTREPRENEURIAL ACTIVITY IN INDIA

Total entrepreneurial activity is the total percentage of the population involved in new business or existing business in the country. Majorly in this section, the following three are discussed; TEA, business ownership, and entrepreneurial employee activity. Data also identifies important nuances for economies where the demographic dividend is the evident impact. In India, data is collected every year to identify entrepreneurship activity amongst various age groups.

The below data table provides unique data points to understand entrepreneurial activity in the country in detail. The first data point nascent entrepreneurs in this table, highlights those people who have recently started or are yet to complete three years. The data shows that 3.2 percent of the surveyed individuals are involved in some kind of new business which is very low, if compared to the perception of opportunity and ease of business in the country.

Another important data point in this table relates to new business owners. The data highlights that 2.3 percent of the surveyed individuals are claiming to be new business owners. Overall 5.3 percent of the population declares that they are engaged in any entrepreneurial activity in the country. The data points are a collective representation of the previous data points.

Table 3.3 TEA, EBA, and EEA in India

Particulars	Rate	Ranking/43
Nascent entrepreneurship	3.2	36
New business ownership	2.3	39
TEA	5.3	39
Establish Business Ownership rate (EBO)	5.9	28
EEA	0.1	43

Source: GEM India Survey 2020-21

Entrepreneurial employee activity is also an important perspective in this analysis. Data identifies that only 0.1 percent of adults in the country perceive that they are contributing to entrepreneurial activity in the country. India ranks 43rd in this and has achieved all other variables in this table. The effect created by pandemic has proved to be difficult for new businesses and these effects can be seen from the emerging low ranking of the country in all the variables discussed above.

Region-wise TEA in India

It is evident in the data that TEA varies within Indian regions. The recent reports of 2019-20 also identified this difference in variations. The difference is majorly caused by the difference in the economic status of the states as well as the entrepreneurial ecosystem in the respective states. Entrepreneurship is praised in certain regions and certain regions meagerly prioritize it. The typical reason for lower TEA in one region and higher in other may be explained by the fact that the western region of the country is more entrepreneurial, more business exists there, industries and work environment is suitable for the new setups, while other regions are half mountainous, or poorer than other regions. There may be many causes for the less involvement of regions in entrepreneurial activity but, entrepreneurship is growing in the country and it is flourishing in the facts discussed in the GEM India snapshots.

To understand the regional differences in the country, it is vital to consider the impact of the ongoing pandemic here. The data highlights a low percentage of respondent's perceiving to be involved in any entrepreneurial activity in the country. The data shows that the highest 2.9 percent of the respondents from the East region perceive that they are involved in some kind of business in their respective region. The data points for the Western region of the country show that 0.9 percent of the population is involved. While it is 1.3 for North it is a meager 0.3 percent for South India. Pandemic has created a great impact on the growth of businesses and led to the closure of many. The impact of this change can be seen easily through this data and by comparing it to other year's data. The proportion of TEA highlighted in the reports is surprisingly different from the current data results. This identifies a changing dynamic of entrepreneurship in the country where regional aspirations are changing and new businesses are emerging throughout.

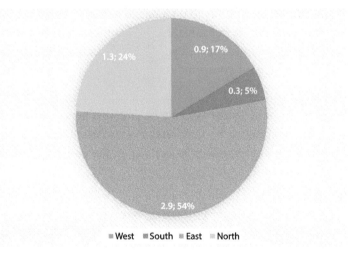

Figure 3.4   Region-wise TEA in India (% of the adult population aged 18-64 years)
Source: *GEM India Survey 2020-21*

TEA Comparison of last four years age groups

In the below figure, data for a comparison of TEA for the last four consecutive years is given. The latest data collected during the ongoing pandemic shows a drastic decrease in performance. The numbers have decreased drastically. The data reflects that total entrepreneurial activity has decreased for all age groups in the country.

The data shows that in 2020-21, only 4 percent of the respondents from India perceive, they are involved in any form of entrepreneurship in the country. The data for the age group 25-36 shows that only 6.6 percent of the population is involved in any kind of entrepreneurial activity this year. For the age group, 35-44, the data shows that only 5.8 percent of the respondents are involved in entrepreneurship of any kind in the country. Data for another senior age group of 45-54 shows that 4.6 percent of the respondents are any way involved in entrepreneurship of any kind in the country. The most senior age group 55-64's data shows that only 4.6 percent of the population is engaged with the entrepreneurship of any kind in the country. The data is clear that pandemic has greatly affected the ongoing entrepreneurial progress in the country. There has been a halt and only a few people could overcome the pandemic and its long-lasting effects. The effect of lockdown and market closure created a great impact upon small and micro-enterprises and this has led to the closure of many businesses in this period. The effect can be seen throughout the economies which participate in the GEM data survey and countries outside the survey.

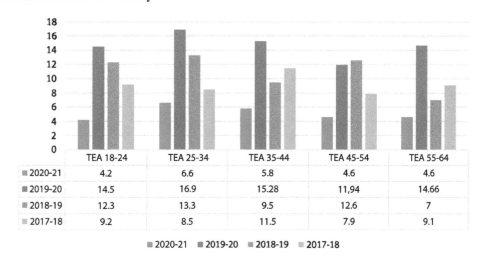

	TEA 18-24	TEA 25-34	TEA 35-44	TEA 45-54	TEA 55-64
■ 2020-21	4.2	6.6	5.8	4.6	4.6
■ 2019-20	14.5	16.9	15.28	11,94	14.66
■ 2018-19	12.3	13.3	9.5	12.6	7
▩ 2017-18	9.2	8.5	11.5	7.9	9.1

■ 2020-21   ■ 2019-20   ■ 2018-19   ▩ 2017-18

Figure 3.5 TEA by age groups in India comparison of last four years
Source: GEM Global Report 2020-21

Gender-wise TEA in Central and East Asian Economies

Total entrepreneurial activity is a significant indicator in this GEM data collected globally. There are various result outcomes. In this table, let us see how East and Central Asian countries perceive TEA in their respective countries. The pandemic is a difficult time as the percentage of male and female TEA has decreased drastically in the countries, represented in the below table. The data shows that less than 10 percent of males and less than eight percent of females are involved in any entrepreneurial activity in the country. The data shown for the other country such as Indonesia, shows that nine percent of males and 10 percent of females are engaged in some kind of entrepreneurial activity. This is important to mention here that females are more into entrepreneurial activity in Indonesia than in any other country. In Kazakhstan, 19 percent of males and 20 percent of females are engaged in some kind of entrepreneurial activity in the country. Here again, more women than men are engaged in entrepreneurial activity. Finally looking into the latest TEA data, it is clear that only 7.9 percent male and a meager number of 2.6 female respondents perceive they are engaged in any entrepreneurial activity in the country. The effect of the pandemic has been everywhere, however, India as a country has faced the most difficult times during pandemic. The closure and lockdown made entrepreneurial adventures difficult. The number in comparison to other countries has decreased drastically and has not produced any good results for the country. The results are depictive of the gender gaps and entrepreneurial capability in these countries. The results also verify a significant need for the improvement of gender inequalities in these societies which seem low in India and the Republic of Korea.

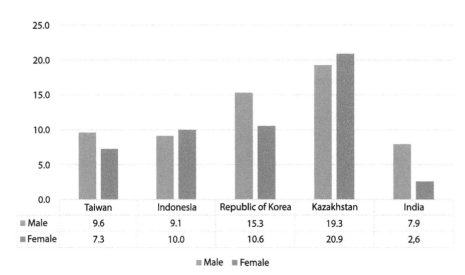

Figure 3.6   TEA in male and female: A East and Central Asian country comparison
Source: *GEM Global Report 2020-21*

Age groups and TEA amongst East and Central Asian economies

People who are in process of either starting a new business or those who already have one and are in the age group of 18 and 64 years, are considered as a part of the total entrepreneurial activity (TEA) in a country. The below data provides a comparison of the entrepreneurial activity between various age groups of 18-64. Looking in the 18-24 age group which is the most ideal age to begin entrepreneurship. The data is predictive of high entrepreneurship in Kazakhstan in this age group. It shows that 18 percent of the people are engaged in entrepreneurial activity (which is the highest percentage of the population engaged in entrepreneurship). Other countries are in the range of 4-8 percent only and India has decreased drastically in the percentage involved in entrepreneurship. The second age group, 25-34 highlights again the effect of Kazakhstan with the highest percentage involved in TEA. India in this age group is again lower than other countries in the list. The confidence has been decreased and people are staying away from the same.

In the third group of 35-44 data shows that 23 percent of Kazakhstan population are involved in TEA, strongly followed by the Republic of Korea with 16 percent and Indonesia with 11 percent. The data also shows statistics for India is very low and only 5.8 percent of the population is involved in a TEA in the country. This is the lowest amongst the countries in this comparison. A low percentage from all the countries perceive that they are engaged in any entrepreneurial activity in the age group of 45-54. This highlights that this age group mostly stays away from starting a new business in any country.

The data for the 55-64 age group is also not satisfactory for many of these countries, especially India. The data declares that Kazakhstan, Republic of Korea are the two high percentage countries with TEA. The data highlights that other countries in this comparison have a very low percentage of the population engaged with entrepreneurial activity. It is important to mention here that entrepreneurship is low and high in different countries. This confirms that old people possess more sources and networks to start a business compared to the young, aged 18-24 in some countries. This gives an important detail of the total entrepreneurial activity in India and also clears that TEA is high in the age group of 25-34 and is expected to rise. It is important to mention here that the entrepreneurship measurement mentioned above includes organizational lifecycle approach i.e. nascent, new business, established business, or nascent entrepreneurs.

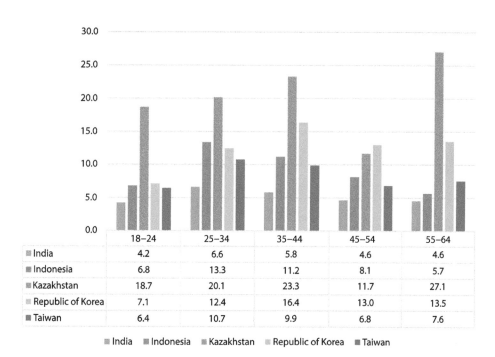

	18–24	25–34	35–44	45–54	55–64
India	4.2	6.6	5.8	4.6	4.6
Indonesia	6.8	13.3	11.2	8.1	5.7
Kazakhstan	18.7	20.1	23.3	11.7	27.1
Republic of Korea	7.1	12.4	16.4	13.0	13.5
Taiwan	6.4	10.7	9.9	6.8	7.6

Figure 3.7   TEA in various population groups in East and Central Asian economies
Source: *GEM Global report 2020-21*

3.3 BUSINESS EXIT AND DISCONTINUATION

The business exit is a critical factor for looking into prospects and it is vital for the entrepreneurship development of a country as well. Business exits and TEA both vary in different economies. Economic condition, personal and finance are the major reasons for discontinuation and exits. People exit either to join or start a venture or to discontinue a business. Both exits and TEA are high in Kazakhstan and followed by the Republic of Korea but Exits are lower in there. The data for India highlights that an equal percentage of the population has exited and confirmed to be a part of TEA in the country.

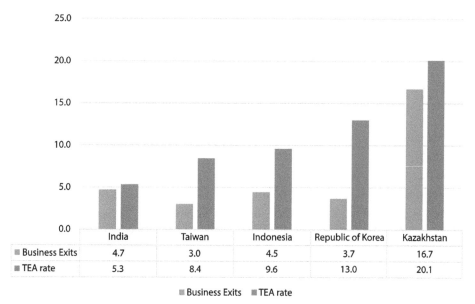

	India	Taiwan	Indonesia	Republic of Korea	Kazakhstan
Business Exits	4.7	3.0	4.5	3.7	16.7
TEA rate	5.3	8.4	9.6	13.0	20.1

Figure 3.8   Business Exit and TEA: A comparison of selected economies
Source: *GEM Global report 2020-21*

3.4 MOTIVATION FOR ENTREPRENEURSHIP

Individual motivation is a primary source of new businesses. In this latest 2020-21 data survey, the questions for motivation are drafted with more clarity and seek answers for what motivates people for entrepreneurship throughout the world. In India motivations for business are majorly due to job scarcity, opportunities, growing market and family reasons. Motivation for entrepreneurial activity depends upon the resource access of an individual (Aldrich & Zimmer, 1986). The table below depicts that global entrepreneurs want to make a difference in the world.80 percent of the total TEA (highest in India) wants to make a difference in the world and followed by Taiwan with 53 percent.

Another important perspective in this series of outcomes is whether entrepreneurs build to make a great wealth or high income out of their business. The data reveals that the highest percent (74%) of Indian adults seek entrepreneurship to build great wealth and increased income. India is followed by Kazakhstan with 95 percent of the population and 68 percent of the republic of Korea population consider wealth creation as a major objective behind their entrepreneurial journey.

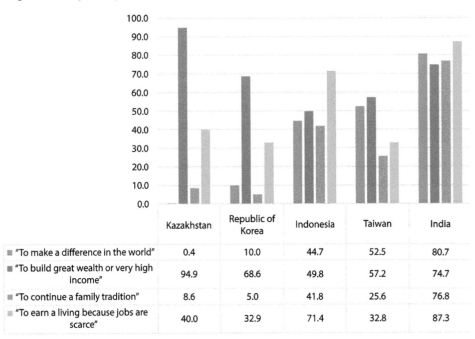

	Kazakhstan	Republic of Korea	Indonesia	Taiwan	India
"To make a difference in the world"	0.4	10.0	44.7	52.5	80.7
"To build great wealth or very high income"	94.9	68.6	49.8	57.2	74.7
"To continue a family tradition"	8.6	5.0	41.8	25.6	76.8
"To earn a living because jobs are scarce"	40.0	32.9	71.4	32.8	87.3

Figure 3.9 Entrepreneurial Motivation: A comparison of Central and East Asia
Source: *GEM Global Report 2020-21*

Existing data and their analysis highlight that many things motivate a person to be an entrepreneur and amongst them going for a family business, making a difference in the world and earning a living due to scarcity of jobs are critical to these factors. Below figure compares various low-income economies based on the survey, for what motivates them to be entrepreneurs. The results in the figure depict that Indians highly perceive that with entrepreneurship they want to make a difference in the world and it is followed by Angola. In the next line, respondents from Togo believe that they want to build a great wealth or high income and that is what motivates them. A high percentage of the respondent from India and Burkina Faso also believe that wealth and high income motivates them.

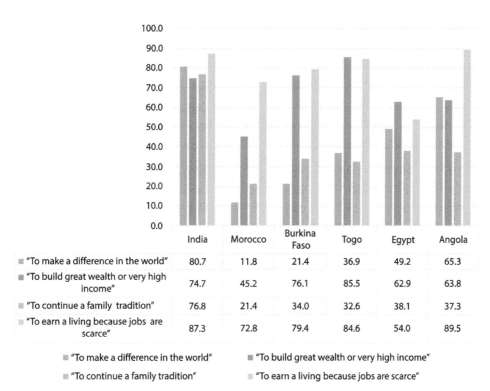

	India	Morocco	Burkina Faso	Togo	Egypt	Angola
▓ "To make a difference in the world"	80.7	11.8	21.4	36.9	49.2	65.3
▓ "To build great wealth or very high income"	74.7	45.2	76.1	85.5	62.9	63.8
▓ "To continue a family tradition"	76.8	21.4	34.0	32.6	38.1	37.3
▓ "To earn a living because jobs are scarce"	87.3	72.8	79.4	84.6	54.0	89.5

▓ "To make a difference in the world" ▓ "To build great wealth or very high income"

▓ "To continue a family tradition" ▓ "To earn a living because jobs are scarce"

Figure 3.10   Entrepreneurial Motivation: A comparison of Low-Income Economies
Source: *GEM Global Report 2020-21*

A high percentage of Indians followed by Egypt, Angola, and Burkina Faso believe that they are motivated to be entrepreneurs by the family tradition. As the global business phenomenon is majorly controlled by family businesses, this is important that young members of the family want to be a part of the legacy. This is the highest in India. Another important outcome of this survey is that people are asked whether job scarcity motivates them to be entrepreneurs. A very high percentage of people from all these countries highlight that they want to be entrepreneurs to overcome job scarcity and to earn a living. It is highest in Angola with 89 percent of the respondents saying yes to it and 87 percent of Indians also believe the same. More than 84 percent of Togo respondents believe the same and it is also high in Burkina Faso and Morocco.

All these data points trigger important understanding that low-income economies face high job scarcity and people want to be entrepreneurs because of that. It also leads to necessity-driven entrepreneurship in a country that is sometimes considered not much impactful. To make entrepreneurship more impactful in these countries it is important to promote innovation-driven entrepreneurship and entrepreneurship for change. It will benefit these countries in the long-term and help them achieve income, change in society, and greater prospects.

3.5 GROWTH EXPECTATION

Growth is very important and helps us identify the prospects of a certain industry or enterprise. Growth is related to employment growth, innovation growth, sales growth, technological progress and others. In GEM methodology, growth expectations are related to the percentage of the 18-64 population, who expect to increase a particular number of employees in the next five years. The growth of jobs and work must encompass population growth, which can lead to economic growth in the country. An increase in jobs in industry and enterprise has a direct relationship to the growth of the economy.

Employment Growth expectation

In this section of the results, the employment growth of the TEA is discussed. The data is a comparison of some participatory countries in a recent GEM survey. The pandemic has hit hard the employment expectation and it can be seen in this data as well. The majority of the surveyed individuals think that they will add 0 jobs to their business till next few years and it is highest amongst the respondents from Kazakhstan and then Indonesia. More than 2 percent of Indians and 9 percent of Kazakhstan respondents believe, they will not add any new employee to their business and the same percentage is high in Taiwan and the Republic of Korea.

The percentage of respondents who want to increase their employment by 1-5 jobs is also very low, but it is lower in India, Taiwan, and Indonesia. The data is clear that around 5 percent each from the Republic of Korea and Kazakhstan expect to increase employment by 1-5 jobs in the next few years. The percentage of TEA who want to increase their employment by more than 6 in the next few years is also high in Kazakhstan, followed by Taiwan and Republic of Korea. The percentage has greatly been affected by the pandemic and it can be seen in the data point in the given figure.

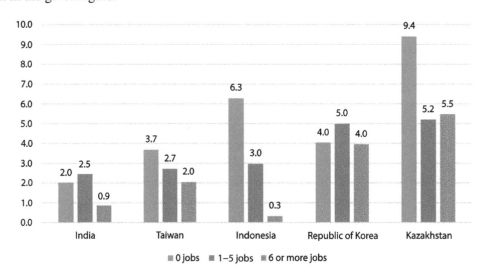

Figure 3.11   Employment projection for the next five years by TEA in India (% of population aged 18-64 years)
Source: *GEM Global Report 2020-21*

3.6 PANDEMIC AND ENTREPRENEURSHIP: A GEM PERSPECTIVE

The World Health Organization declared a new pandemic called Covid-19, on 11th March 2020. Since then, the world has been witnessing lockdowns, deaths, business closures and income losses. The pandemic hit every sector and rate of job losses rose very high in the first two quarters and it also led to labor migration and labor loss. This long-term process is taking time to settle down and it is difficult to say when the world will start working normally, as it used to do before the pandemic. The pandemic effect is very strong and in the below figure, the overall effect of a pandemic on business in Central and East Asia is discussed.

Impact of Covid-19 on Enabling Factors

In this chapter, it has been continuously observed that pandemic has greatly impacted the businesses and entrepreneurship in most of the countries, including India. The enabling factors in the country have dropped in percentage from last year. However, not all the factors have been effected. Perceived opportunity has not been much effected. It shows that people are still confident that opportunities are available in their area and more than

81 of the respondents believe, they possess knowledge and skill to perceive entrepreneurship. Fear of failure amongst people has increased by 1 percent and more than 56 percent of the people fear failure while starting a new business. The major effect can be seen on entrepreneurial intention of the individuals. There has been a 39 percent change and only 20 percent of the population has an intention to become entrepreneurs even if they possess capability and there are opportunities in the country as well. The expectation to start a new business has also gone down and only 22 percent of the population expects to start a new business in next 3 years.

Table 3.4 Enabling factors in India a comparison

Enabling Factors	2019-20	2020-21	Difference
Perceived opportunity	83.14	82.45	(0.84%)
Perceived capability	85.15	81.65	(4.11%)
Fear of failure	55.94	56.8	(1.53%)
Entrepreneurial Intention	33.30	20.31	(39.01%)
Expects to start-up in the next 3 years	34.91	22.42	(35.79%)

Source: APS survey 2020-21

Pandemic and Entrepreneurial activity a comparison

Pandemic has affected every aspect of business in most of the countries. By looking at the below statistics, it becomes clear that there has been a huge impact of covid-19 over the entrepreneurial activity in the country. Nascent entrepreneurship in the country decreased from 9.44 to 3.17 in 2020-21. There has been a decline of 66 percent. Another important variable, new entrepreneur's rate, has also decreased from 5.90 to 2.27 in these two years. The data figure also shows a high decrease in total entrepreneurial activity from last year. The change has been recorded at 64 percent decreasing from 15 in 2019-20 to 5.34 in 2020-21.

Another important aspect of entrepreneurial activity is male versus female entrepreneurial activity. In both cases, total entrepreneurial activity has decreased by 53 for male and 79 percent for females. The data also shows statistics for established business ownership rates. The data highlights that businesses which are 42 months older, have also decreased in number. The percentage of established business has changed from 11.92 percent to 5.88 percent. It shows new business ownership rate has decreased by 50 percent in the past one year.

Table 3.5 Change in the entrepreneurial activity due to pandemic

Particulars	2019-20	2020-21	Difference
Nascent Entrepreneurs rate (0 to 6 Years)	9.44	3.17	(66.42%)
New Entrepreneurs rate (up to 42 Months)	5.90	2.27	(61.51%)
Total Entrepreneurship Activity (TEA)	15.00	5.34	(64.40%)
Total Entrepreneurship Activity Male	17.10	7.94	(53.58%)
Total Entrepreneurship Activity Female	12.74	2.62	(79.44%)
Established Business rate (More than 42 Months old)	11.92	5.88	(50.66%)

Source: APS Survey 2020-21

Knowing someone who has started, or stopped, a business due to the pandemic

During the current APS survey, the respondents throughout the world, were asked whether they know someone who started or stopped a business during the pandemic and particularly due to the pandemic. The results can be seen in the below figure which highlights that the highest number of respondents from Indonesia (72 percent), declare that they know someone who stopped a business and 69 percent perceive they know someone who started a new business. It shows that an equal proportion of businesses got closed and started during the pandemic.

Another important outcome of this result is that 53 percent of Indians perceive they know someone who started a new business and a slightly high proportion of 60 percent of the respondents, perceive that they know someone who stopped a business during a pandemic. This is an important outcome that more than half of the business stopped working and alternatively more than half started afresh. In the same line, it can be seen that around 60 percent of the Kazakhstan respondents believe that they know someone who stopped a business and they know less than 10 percent who started a new business during the pandemic. The percentage of these respondents is lower in Taiwan and the Republic of Korea.

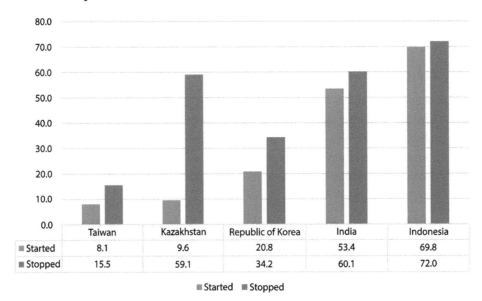

	Taiwan	Kazakhstan	Republic of Korea	India	Indonesia
■ Started	8.1	9.6	20.8	53.4	69.8
■ Stopped	15.5	59.1	34.2	60.1	72.0

■ Started ■ Stopped

Figure 3.12   Percentage of people who know someone who started or stooped a business during the pandemic
Source: *GEM data survey 2020-21*

Pandemic and delay in business operational

The coronavirus led to long-duration lockdowns in the biggest economies of the world and in India, the lockdown was also long and hectic. The long pause in the business operation led to operational delays and the same is discussed in the below figure. The data shows that the operational delays have been of different levels and respondents in India, Kazakhstan, and Taiwan perceive that pandemic has led to a delay in getting business operational. Data shows that more than 84 percent of the people in India perceive pandemic has delayed the business operations in the country and the same is perceived by nearly 83 percent in Kazakhstan. The pandemic led to delay in business operations is perceived by 73 percent of the respondents from Taiwan and 55 percent from Indonesia.

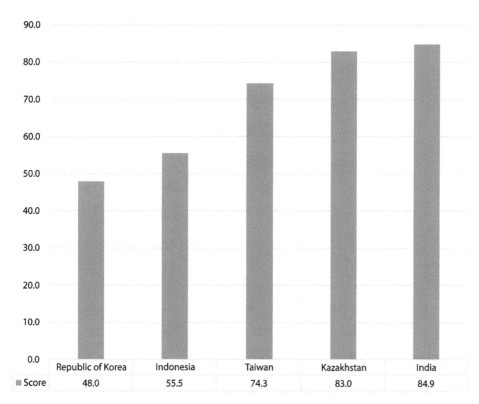

	Republic of Korea	Indonesia	Taiwan	Kazakhstan	India
■ Score	48.0	55.5	74.3	83.0	84.9

Figure 3.13   Business operations delay due to pandemic
Source: *GEM data survey 2020-21*

Pandemic and new business opportunities

The below data highlights the perception of respondents regarding pandemics and its effects on new business creation. The respondents from Central and East economies are a part of this data result. The results show that the highest 13 percent of the respondents from Kazakhstan perceive that they do not see any new opportunities coming up due to pandemic compared to only 5 percent who perceive that they see new opportunities coming up. The results vary for other countries in these data points. The data shows that more than 12 percent of the respondents from the Republic of Korea perceive they do not find any new opportunity due to the Covid-19 pandemic and 1 percent believe they do see new opportunities.

It is only in India where the perception of the people is different from the other countries. The data shows that 3.4 percent of the respondents believe that they find some opportunity in the country and less than 2 percent think otherwise. The data points highlight that Indians are more positive regarding business opportunities in inappropriate times than respondents in any other country. The data points also show the confidence in the population over the working of the government and control over the disease in the country.

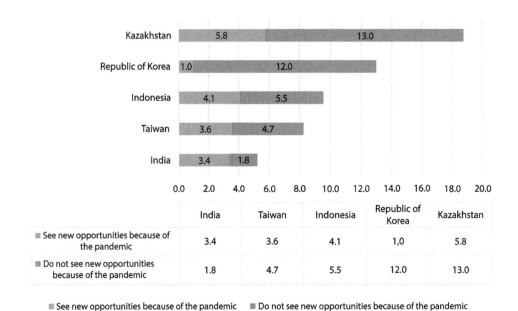

	India	Taiwan	Indonesia	Republic of Korea	Kazakhstan
▣ See new opportunities because of the pandemic	3.4	3.6	4.1	1,0	5.8
▣ Do not see new opportunities because of the pandemic	1.8	4.7	5.5	12.0	13.0

▣ See new opportunities because of the pandemic   ▣ Do not see new opportunities because of the pandemic

Figure 3.14   Level of Tea and Business opportunities
Source: *GEM data survey 2020-21*

Impact of the pandemic on household income (% of adults aged 18–64 in each category)

The sudden occurrence of the pandemic created havoc not only on the poor of the poorest, but also upon the middle class, working-class, businesses and other groups. The lockdown shut the door of income for a large part of the global population. The lockdown has been of varying durations in different countries and led to the shutting down of millions of businesses. The effect of pandemic upon household income has been very high as shown in the below data figure. The data shows that respondents from most of the countries share equal perceptions regarding the impact of pandemics on their household income.

Around 44 percent of the Indians perceive that pandemic has strongly affected their household income, 37 percent from Kazakhstan, around 22 percent of Indonesians and 16 percent of the Taiwan.

The major proportion from all these countries in the table believes that pandemic has somewhat affected their household income. The data shows that 57 percent of respondents from Indonesia, 55 percent in Kazakhstan, 42 percent in India perceive that pandemic has hit their household income.

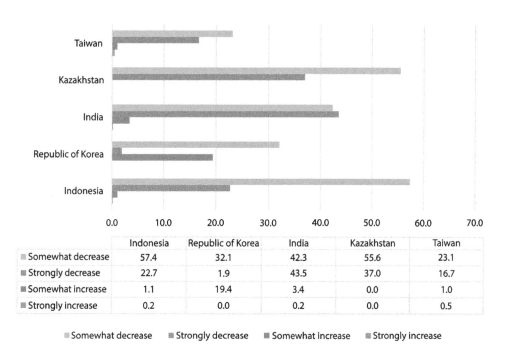

	Indonesia	Republic of Korea	India	Kazakhstan	Taiwan
▪ Somewhat decrease	57.4	32.1	42.3	55.6	23.1
▪ Strongly decrease	22.7	1.9	43.5	37.0	16.7
▪ Somewhat increase	1.1	19.4	3.4	0.0	1.0
▪ Strongly increase	0.2	0.0	0.2	0.0	0.5

▪ Somewhat decrease   ▪ Strongly decrease   ▪ Somewhat increase   ▪ Strongly increase

Figure 3.15   Impact of a pandemic on household income
Source: GEM data survey 2020-21

Some respondents also perceive that their income somewhat increased during the pandemic. Around 19 percent of the respondents from the Republic of Taiwan believe that their income increased during the pandemic. The data also shows that the respondents from other countries in Central and East Asia do not perceive their income increased during the pandemic. Less than 1 percent of respondents from all the countries in the data table highlight that their income increased strongly during the pandemic time.

SUMMARY

COVID-19 pandemic has a significant Impact on Entrepreneurship Activities and its related dimensions. Female entrepreneurship activity rate is severely affected by the pandemic and effect is seen to be stronger in developing world, where a big chunk of population earn and lives on daily basis. The businesses were shut and employment was drastically decreased in this process. The pandemic created varied impact over the business community including MSME, retail and corporates. The effect of pandemic is going to stay as the new normal. The requirement is for new strategies to adopt to this new normal for which digital initiatives, work from home and prevention are important part.

Entrepreneurship Framework Conditions in India : National Expert Survey (NES)

4

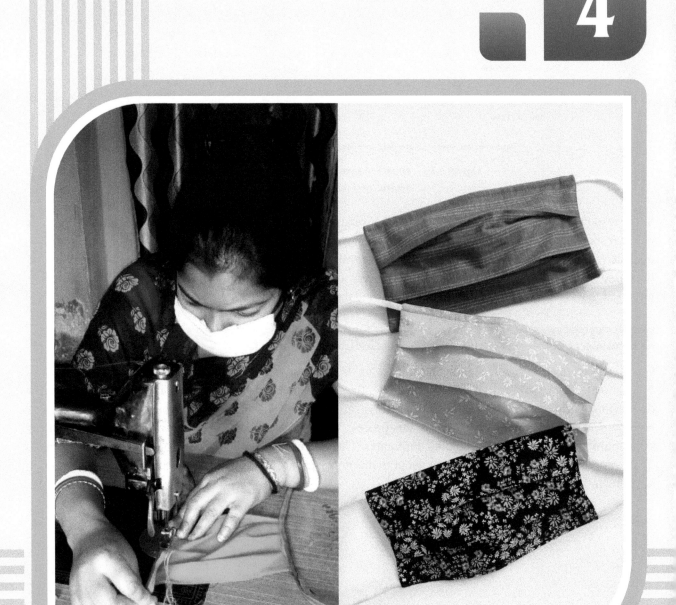

OVERVIEW

An ecosystem is built by various factors and parameters that individually, as well as collectively, impact the wholeness of that ecosystem. Likewise, an entrepreneurial ecosystem is fabricated by many strings. Since its initiation, GEM, has focused on the conditions that enhance (or hinder) the new business creation. Considering this, GEM has proposed some parameters to analyse their effect on the entrepreneurship ecosystem, termed as, *Entrepreneurship Framework Conditions*. These conditions directly influence the entrepreneurial opportunities, entrepreneurial capacity and entrepreneurial preferences. Entrepreneurial Framework Conditions vary across different regions and economies and hence, requires the analysis as per the context of the place and surroundings. Currently, there are nine major dimensions that define Entrepreneurial Framework. Figure 4.1 discloses these dimensions.

Figure 4.1   Entrepreneurial Framework Conditions

Source: *About National Expert Survey, GEM*

4.1 ENTREPRENEURIAL FRAMEWORK CONDITIONS IN INDIA

While analysing the Entrepreneurial Framework Conditions in India, some of the major factors, further get split into two parameters, for a better and holistic understanding of that dimension. This creates a comprehensive list of twelve factors, namely; access to entrepreneurial finance, government policy: support and relevance, government policy: taxes and bureaucracy, entrepreneurship education at school, entrepreneurship at post-schools, research and development transfers, commercial and professional infrastructure, ease of entry: market burden and regulations, physical infrastructure, and social and cultural norms.

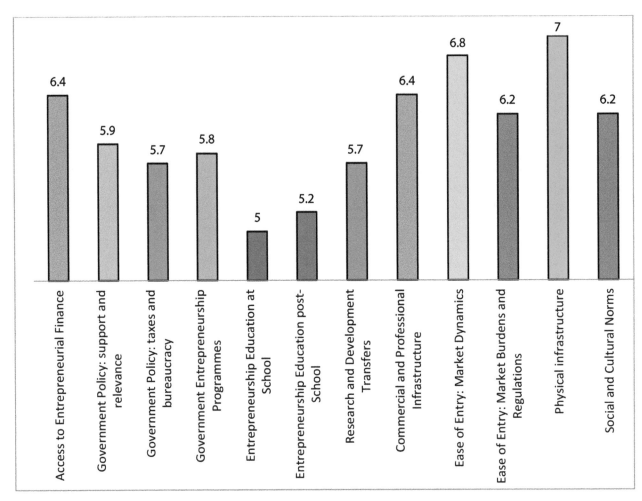

Figure 4.2 Entrepreneurial framework conditions of India
Source: *GEM India Survey*

Overall, India bagged 6th place in the list of economies. Eventually, India has improved on many grounds. Every year, the country is adding on, across all twelve pillars for a renovated and enhanced entrepreneurial ecosystem. Physical infrastructure and ease of entry for market burden and regulations are the most progressive conditions in India, followed by commercial and professional infrastructure and access to entrepreneurial finance. Though the entrepreneurial ecosystem of the nation is amplifying by time, still, there are a few dimensions that seek attention; like, entrepreneurship education at school and post-school.

As per the annual analysis of the country, India has put a lot of efforts on two parameters; access to entrepreneurial finance and easy of entry. It has also improved the government taxes and bureaucracy policies, research and development transfers, commercial and professional infrastructure, physical infrastructure and social and cultural norms, when compared with previous year. In fact, India is at first place in overall economic ranking for access to entrepreneurial finance and second and third for ease of entry for market burdens and regulations and research & development, respectively. Further, when compared to the last year's ranking, India has slipped few steps in entrepreneurship education, government entrepreneurship programmes and government policy for support and relevance, indicating larger scope of improvement.

4.2 ENTREPRENEURSHIP FRAMEWORK CONDITIONS: COMPARISON OF LOW-INCOME COUNTRIES

The GEM India 2020-21 survey has analysed the entrepreneurship framework conditions of five low income countries, which include; India, Angola, Burkina Faso, Togo and Morocco. Through this analysis, we can make a better comparison of low income economies ecosystem. This would give a clearer picture about the position of Indian ecosystem among the developing countries.

Out of these low income economies, India has been tremendously good as an entrepreneurial ecosystem. India is a leading ecosystem for entrepreneurs as compared to the other low income economies, across all pillars of framework conditions. All these economies are very focused towards the physical infrastructure and access to entrepreneurial finance. One factor, which is least developed, is entrepreneurship education at school. Though in comparison to the other economies, India has made strenuous efforts on entrepreneurship education in schools. India has created a major difference with other low income economies, in context to research and development transfers. Where other economies are majorly focused on physical infrastructure and market dynamics, India is investing on research and development to enhance its entrepreneurial ecosystem in a holistic way.

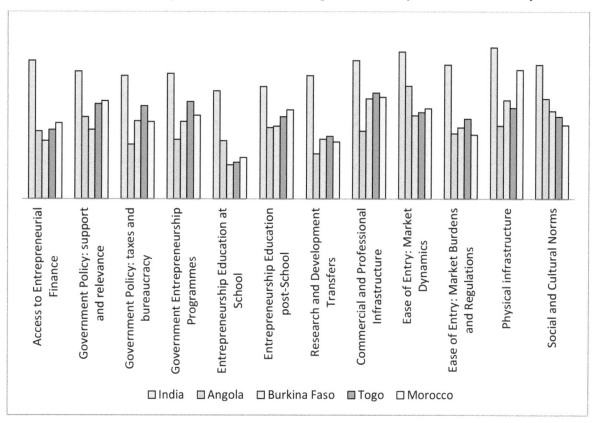

Figure 4.3 Entrepreneurial framework conditions of Low-Income countries
Source: GEM India Survey

4.3 ENTREPRENEURIAL FRAMEWORK CONDITIONS: CENTRAL AND EAST ASIA

Amongst the Central and East Asian economies, this report is focused on five economies, namely; India, Taiwan, Indonesia, Republic of Korea and Kazakhstan. Again, this analysis provides a comparison about the entrepreneurial ecosystem of India against other Central and East Asian economies. Overall, the status of entrepreneurial ecosystem of India is appreciable in comparison with economies.

According to the ranking, Indonesia has a very impressive contribution across five conditions for an improved entrepreneurial ecosystem. Amongst these five economies, India bags first place for access to entrepreneurial finance, commercial and professional infrastructure and ease of entry: market burdens and regulations. Taiwan has surpassed in context to government policy support and relevance. In context to taxes and bureaucracy, entrepreneurship education, research and development, and social and cultural norms, Indonesia has best ecosystem amongst the five. Government entrepreneurship programmes are best handled by Taiwan along with physical infrastructure. Republic of Korea has rigorously worked on ease of entry: market dynamics.

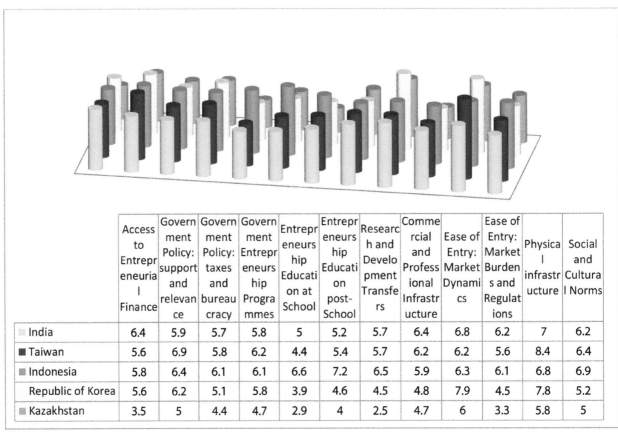

	Access to Entrepreneurial Finance	Government Policy: support and relevance	Government Policy: taxes and bureaucracy	Government Entrepreneurship Programmes	Entrepreneurship Education at School	Entrepreneurship Education post-School	Research and Development Transfers	Commercial and Professional Infrastructure	Ease of Entry: Market Dynamics	Ease of Entry: Market Burdens and Regulations	Physical infrastructure	Social and Cultural Norms
India	6.4	5.9	5.7	5.8	5	5.2	5.7	6.4	6.8	6.2	7	6.2
Taiwan	5.6	6.9	5.8	6.2	4.4	5.4	5.7	6.2	6.2	5.6	8.4	6.4
Indonesia	5.8	6.4	6.1	6.1	6.6	7.2	6.5	5.9	6.3	6.1	6.8	6.9
Republic of Korea	5.6	6.2	5.1	5.8	3.9	4.6	4.5	4.8	7.9	4.5	7.8	5.2
Kazakhstan	3.5	5	4.4	4.7	2.9	4	2.5	4.7	6	3.3	5.8	5

Figure 4.4   Entrepreneurial framework conditions of Central and East Asia

Source: *GEM India Survey*

4.4 ENTREPRENEURSHIP FINANCING IN INDIA

Entrepreneurship financing as a framework condition, concentrates on availability of financial resources for entrepreneurs, both equity and debt. This includes all grants and subsidies. In India, the financial ecosystem for entrepreneurs is highly favourable. Every year, the country is putting a lot of resources to strongly back the financial ecosystem of the country. This parameter has further eight dimensions, which try to analyse equity funding, debt funding, government subsidies, funding from private individuals, business angels, venture capitalists, initial public offerings and crowd funding. Amongst all these, venture capitalists parameter, is their strongest dimension, followed by informal and private individuals like; family and friends. As compared to previous year, the ecosystem has improved across all dimensions. The maximum enhancement is observed in initial public offerings, business angels and equity funding.

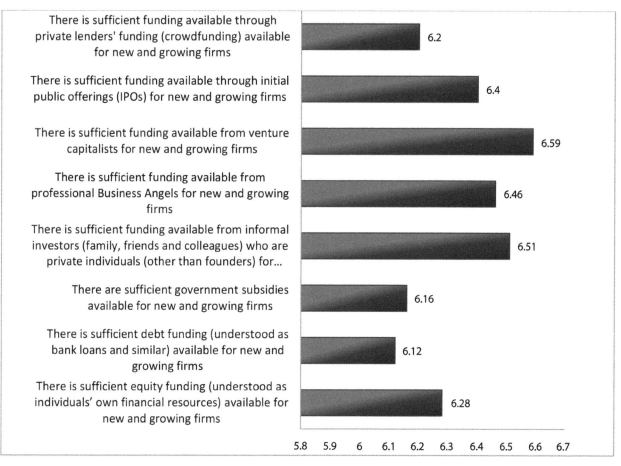

Figure 4.5   Entrepreneurship Financing in India
Source: *GEM India Survey*

4.5 GOVERNMENT SUPPORT AND POLICIES IN INDIA

Government policies emphasise on the support that the entrepreneurs get through the public policies. It is examined on the basis of what extent these policies are supporting the enterprises. The parameter is further divided on the basis of four dimensions. The most appreciated dimension is the government policies for public procurement, legislation, regulation, licensing, taxation that would consistently favour new firms.

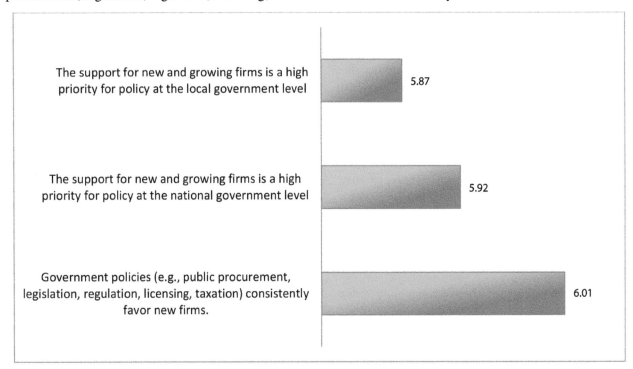

Figure 4.6 Government Support and Policies in India
Source: *GEM India Survey*

In comparison with the last year, all dimensions show improvement, except the national level support priority for new and growing firms. The score of this area has skipped by 0.4 points. Still, national level support is stronger than the local government support. Local governments need to take major steps to facilitate a favourable ecosystem to their entrepreneurs.

4.6 TAXES AND BUREAUCRACY IN INDIA

Taxes and bureaucracy are the second component of government policy as a whole. This aspect takes care of taxes and regulations that would support the new as well as growing firms. The parameter has further four angels through which it is evaluated. According to the analysis of the GEM experts, the taxes are the government regulations that are applied in a very predictable and consistent way. This is the strongest angel of taxes and bureaucracy. Further, there is an ease in coping with government bureaucracy, regulations and licensing requirements. Though there is a lot of scope for improvement in permit and licenses along with tax burden. The two are favourable but a little improvement would be more encouraging for the entrepreneurs.

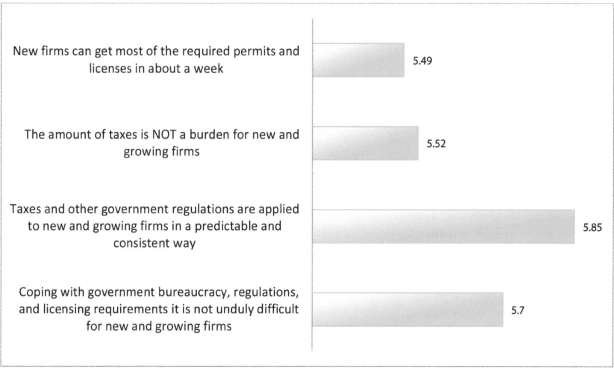

Figure 4.7 Taxes and Bureaucracy in India
Source: *GEM India Survey*

4.7 GOVERNMENT PROGRAMMES IN INDIA

At Central as well as local level, the government gets involved in various entrepreneurship programmes. Both the levels conduct programmes at central as well as local level, to help the new and growing businesses with different kind of proficiency and skill enhancement. The experts analyse this area with the help of six parameters. Overall, government programmes are doing very well in providing a favourable ecosystem to the entrepreneurs. Most importantly, there is adequate count of government programmes along with the support from business incubators and science parks. Government is taking adequate steps to support entrepreneurs from diverse industries. Though, the government can add more expertise in the programmes organised by them. As compared to the previous year's performance, the government is aiming more at supporting the new and growing firms. Government has also worked on the expertise in the programme that would train the entrepreneurs and support them by enhancing their skills.

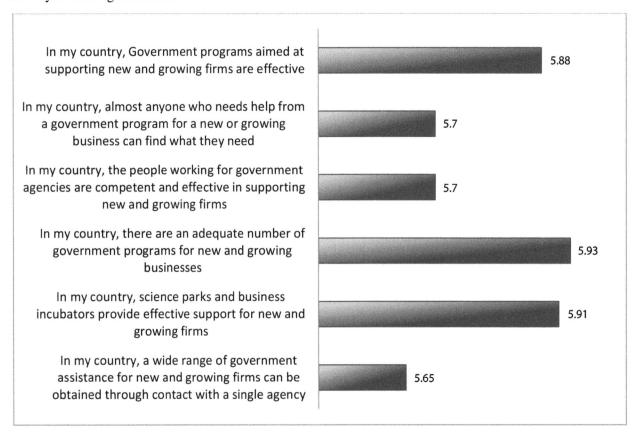

Figure 4.8 Government Programmes in India
Source: GEM India Survey

4.8 EDUCATION – PRIMARY AND SECONDARY

The entrepreneurial education focuses on the training for creation and managing the enterprise. It has two components. One component is focused on education at basic school level (primary and secondary), whereas, the other focuses on post-secondary level (higher education such as vocational, college, business schools, etc.).

Figure 4.9 displays the scores of first component – basic school level entrepreneurship education in India. When we compare the entrepreneurial education with other twelve conditions, there is still a lot to be done. Though, India has worked better than many developing countries. In fact India stands at rank one when compared with some developing countries. Experts analyse school level education through three dimensions. According to expert survey, education is surely enhancing the creativity, self-sufficiency and personal initiative aspects among the students. Though, there is a need for a lot of efforts, when it comes to adequate attention for entrepreneurship and new firm creation. Compared to the last year, the entrepreneurial education in primary and secondary level has taken a rise.

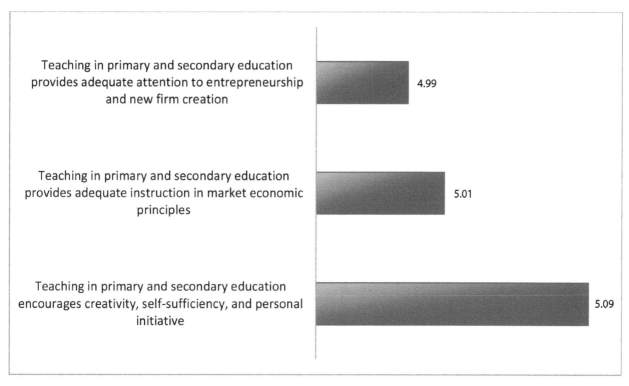

Figure 4.9   Education (Primary and Secondary) in India
Source: *GEM India Survey*

4.9 EDUCATION – POST SECONDARY LEVEL IN INDIA

The figure 4.10 describes the second component of entrepreneurial education, dealing with the post-secondary level education. Compared with primary and secondary level education, the overall position of post-secondary level in India is superior. These programmes are very well focused on the adequate preparation of vocational and professional entrepreneurial education. Further, the quality of education is well maintained. Compared to the previous year, the post-secondary institutes need to push themselves forward. But, when compared with other developed countries scoring, India is doing very well in entrepreneurship education.

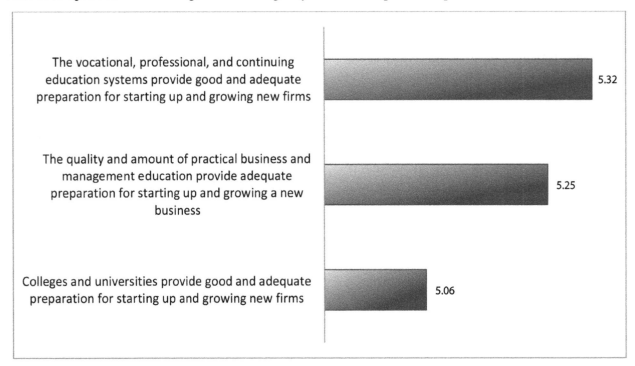

Figure 4.10   Education (Post-secondary level) in India

Source: *GEM India Survey*

4.10 COMMERCIAL AND LEGAL INFRASTRUCTURE IN INDIA

Commercial and legal infrastructure is concentrated with the presence of property rights and other related legal services that support the new and growing firms. India has been doing tremendously good on these grounds. Comparing with the last year, this year, we can observe a considerable up-liftment, as per the expert scoring. For overall assessment, the experts analyse through five different aspects. In all the five areas, India has a favourable ecosystem. Most favourable aspect is that it is very easy for new and growing firms to get good banking services along with the legal and accounting services. The maximum improvement is observed in affordability for subcontractors, supplier and consultant, followed by quality of subcontractors, supplier and consultants.

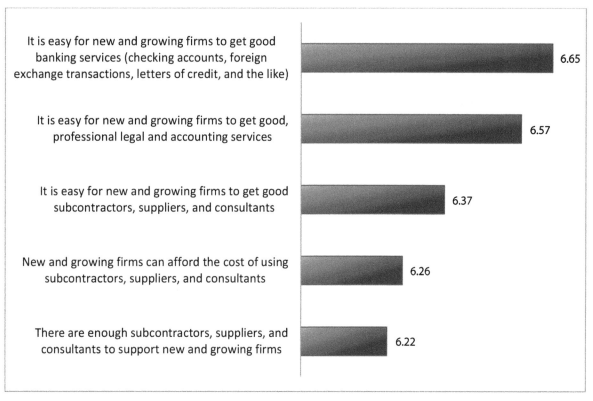

Figure 4.11   Commercial and Legal Infrastructure in India
Source: *GEM India Survey*

4.11 INTERNAL MARKET DYNAMICS IN INDIA

GEM experts have divided the entry regulations in two parts. Figure 4.12 is focusing on one part; i.e. market dynamics. Through market dynamics, experts study the level of change in the market, from one year to another. Further dynamics are analysed on two parameters; business-to-business dynamics and consumer goods and service market dynamics. As one of the framework condition, India has a good ecosystem in context to internal market dynamics. Though, business-to-business change dynamics is more progressive as compared to consumer market. Compared with last year, the dynamics has really improved further. We can think of more developed ecosystem for consumer market.

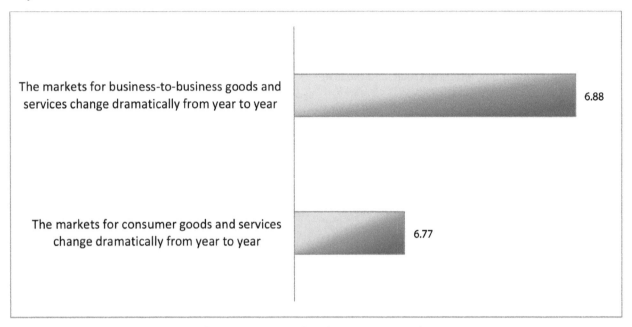

Figure 4.12   Internal Market Dynamics in India
Source: *GEM India Survey*

4.12 INTERNAL MARKET OPENNESS IN INDIA

This is the second aspect of entry regulation, i.e. market openness. This is used to analyse the extent, to which the new firms are free to enter existing markets. For analyses, this parameter is studied by reviewing four factors as shown in figure 4.13. Overall, the condition is favourable for entrepreneurs, indicating an easy entry for new firms. The ecosystem is advantageous, when we talk affording cost of entry by new firms. India is also working well on the unfair blocks by established firms.

As compared to the last year's scoring, Indian ecosystem has improved multi-fold in internal dynamics. We can observe a lot of positive differences created across different factors. The maximum variation is done in the affordability of cost to enter the market by new firms. This is a crucial factor that would ease the entry of new and young entrepreneurs. One factor which needs attention is the effective and well enforced anti-trust legislation. This factor scores little less when compared to other factors of internal market openness and the score has also slipped by some points compared to last year.

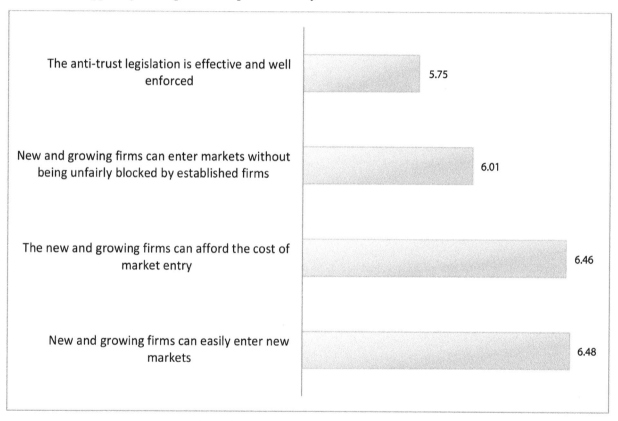

Figure 4.13   Internal Market Openness in India
Source: *GEM India Survey*

4.13 PHYSICAL INFRASTRUCTURE IN INDIA

Under this framework condition, experts study about how easily the entrepreneurs are able to access the physical resources. Here physical resources include communication, utilities, transportation, land or space at a non-discriminated price. Till last year, this analysis was done on the basis of five factors. But in 2020-21, these factors have increased to seven. Figure 4.14 displays all seven factors with their scores for this year. Affordable productive space and office space, are the two newly added parameters that are studied and analysed by the experts for the overall understanding of physical infrastructure ecosystem in India.

Out of all the framework conditions, this is one of the outstanding condition in Indian entrepreneurial ecosystem. All dimensions of this condition are equally favourable for entrepreneurs. The most favourable factor is the count of affordable office space for new and growing firms, followed by easy access to physical communication and affordability factor of all basic utilities. The other factors are adding in a perfect way to make it beneficial for the entrepreneurs. One factor that could be improved, is the support that an entrepreneur could get through physical infrastructure. Comparing with last year, all factors have improved except communication and access to utilities.

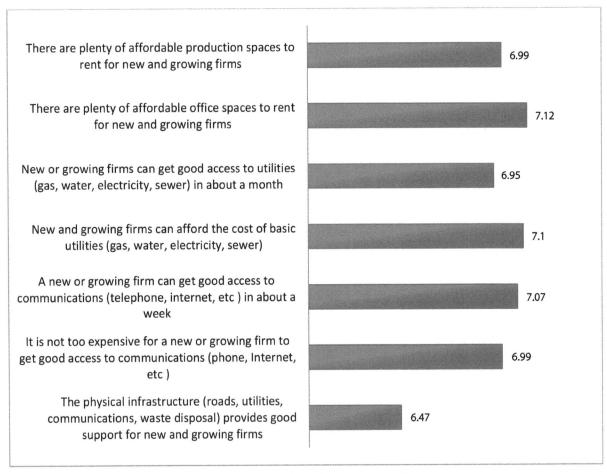

Figure 4.14   Physical Infrastructure in India

Source: *GEM India Survey*

4.14 RESEARCH AND DEVELOPMENT IN INDIA

Under research and development, we could understand, up to what extent, the research and development of the nation could create commercial opportunities for the entrepreneurs. The analysis is done on the basis of six different factors by the experts. The overall strength of this framework condition is averagely good as compared to other conditions.

The most beneficial factor is that the engineers and scientists get enough support to commercialise their ideas through new and growing firms. This is an advantageous factor for entrepreneurs in context of the growth, development and survival of their business. Other factors are adding as a beneficiary factor. A comprehensive picture could be seen in figure 4.15. When compared with the previous year's score, this year the research and development has improved in many aspects. Except one, all the other factors, show a considerable growth in their scores. The most improved factors are, access to new research and technology by the firms, affordability of latest technologies by the firms and support of government subsidies to acquire new technology by the new and growing firms.

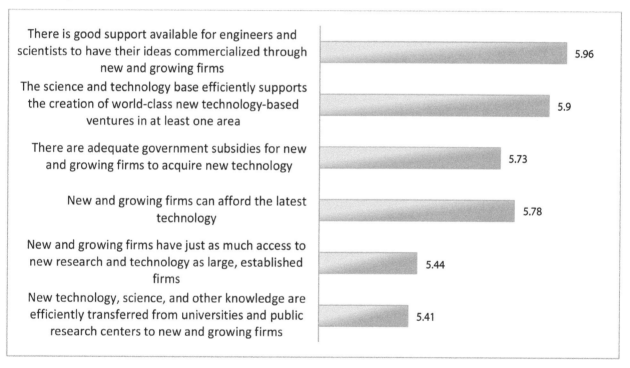

Figure 4.15   Research and Development in India
Source: GEM India Survey

4.15 SOCIAL AND CULTURAL NORMS IN INDIA

This condition takes care of the social and cultural norms that encourage the new business methods and activities that would help in increasing personal wealth and income. The analysis is done through five different factors. Altogether, this framework condition is contributing very well in making the ecosystem favourable for the entrepreneurs. The most positive aspect is that the national culture of the country emphasis the responsibility towards the individual in managing his or her own life. There has been an increase in the expert scoring across various factors, when compared to the last year's scores. The major shift has been observed in cultural emphasise on individual responsibility. Though, there is slit reduction in the scores of two factors. These factors concern the encouragement of culture for creativity and innovation and emphasis on self-sufficiency, autonomy and personal initiative.

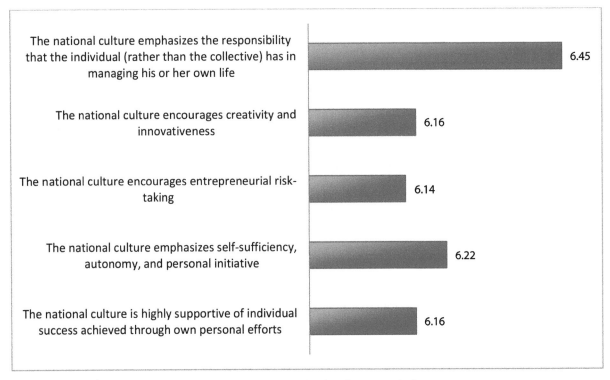

Figure 4.16   Social and Cultural Norms in India
Source: *GEM India Survey*

4.16 EXPERTS' ASSESSMENT OF RESPONSES TO THE PANDEMIC

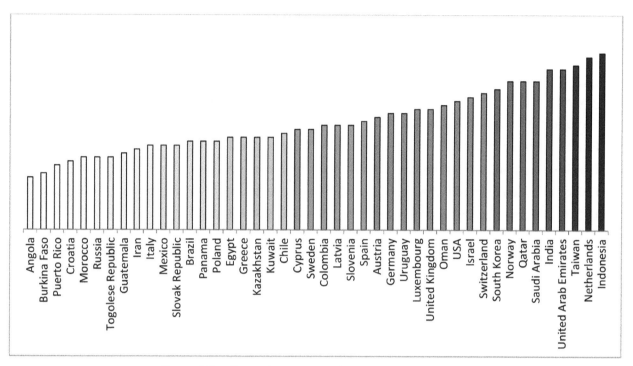

Figure 4.17   Experts' Assessment of Response to the Pandemic
Source: *GEM India Survey*

2020-21 has been a difficult time for the economies across the globe. Due to the pandemic, every sector had to absorb the shocks of the market. Though, countries have tried to handle the situation through various supports. Governments have played the most crucial role in supporting different sectors, which further helped in recovery of the economy. Figure 4.16 represents the assessment by the experts considering the situation of pandemic. Countries like; Angola, Burkina Faso, Puerto Rico and Croatia are at the bottom five, indicating the scope of a lot of improvement in their entrepreneurial ecosystem. In addition to this, even Russia fell in amongst the least ten economies. The top five ranked economies by the experts are: Indonesia, Netherlands, Taiwan, United Arab Emirates and India.

India has worked hard at the time of pandemic to recover its economic losses. Because of these efforts, the country was able to have a V-shaped recovery. This rapid recovery could be possible with the efforts of government and active responses by various industries. The Government of India, took timely and effective steps, to support the entrepreneurs. This government support helped the firms to survive and handle their losses. *Atmanirbhar Bharat*, was the biggest encouragement for the entrepreneurs and various sectors, to persist in such market conditions. On 12 May 2020, the Hon'ble Prime Minister of India, announced about the Atmanirbhar Bharat (Self-reliant India campaign), which was an endowment for the nation. Under this scheme, a special economic and comprehensive package of INR 20 lakh crore was provided to fight the COVID-19 pandemic in India. The package was equivalent to the 10% GDP of the country. The funds were distributed among five pillars: economy, infrastructure, system, vibrant demography and demand. The scheme was very beneficial for the businesses. Through this scheme, businesses were able to access collateral free loans, increase in borrowing limit, credit boost to farmers, subordinate debt for MSMEs and schemes for street vendors. For entrepreneurs a package was released, which included the following:

❏ INR 3 lakh crore collateral-free automatic loans for businesses, including MSMEs.

❏ INR 20,000 crore subordinate debt for stressed MSMEs

❏ INR 50,000 crore equity infusion for MSMEs through fund of Funds

❏ Low threshold in MSME definition created fear among MSMEs of graduating out of the benefits. Therefore government revised the definition of MSMEs.

❏ Global tenders were disallowed upto INR 200 crores

❏ E-market linkage for MSMEs as a replacement for trade fairs and exhibitions

❏ INR 2500 crore support for business & workers for 3 more months

❏ EPF contribution reduced for business & workers for 3 months – INR 6750 crores liquidity support

❏ INR 30,000 crore special liquidity scheme for NBFCs/ HFCs/ MFIs

❏ INR 45,000 crore partial credit guarantee scheme 2.0 for NBFCs

❏ INR 90,000 credit liquidity injection for DISCOMs

❏ Relief Contractors

❏ Extension of registration and completion date of real estate projects under RERA

❏ INR 50,000 crore liquidity through TDS/ TCS rate reduction

The support was not only facilitated through financial support, but the government of India, also focused on other parameters like, regulatory reforms and investors engagement. The government has reformed the tax regulations by extending the last date of tax returns. Along with this, the GST filling was extended. Ministry of Corporate Affairs, introduced "Companies Fresh Start Scheme, 2020" and "LLPs Settlement Scheme, 2020" to support the companies and LLPs. Even SEBI and RBI had relaxed some norms to provide ease to the entrepreneurs. Parallel to this, the states have also taken initiatives to support in economic recovery. Initiatives like, Q-city and T-HUB in Hyderabad along with Centre for Cellular and Molecular Platforms (C-CAMP) have been successfully advantageous to fight COVID in India.

Conclusion and Policy Suggestions

5

Entrepreneurship has become a key factor of sustainable economic growth and has huge potential to create employment opportunities. Developing an entrepreneurial mindset within the country, has become a key objective for governments and societies worldwide. In the Indian context, given its socio-economic challenges as well as its size and scope, a holistic approach to entrepreneurship development, can bring transformational changes to the socio-economic landscape. Adopting a simplified common approach or simply following an existing model of entrepreneurship development (even if it is highly successful elsewhere), will not help India to achieve its potential. What is needed is a holistic model of pervasive entrepreneurship development, driven by innovations and values that can address India's unique challenges.

The GEM India 2020-21 report, unveils the entrepreneurial activities in the country. This report provides data and analysis that can help academicians, researchers, policymakers and professionals to take appropriate action for enhancing economic growth, with a focus on broad-based entrepreneurship development. Another significant contribution is that, it enables us to assess how the entrepreneurial activity and profiles change in the time of the COVID-19 pandemic. The report examined key aspects of the entrepreneurship amongst Indians, by measuring their attitudes, activities and aspirations. The findings of the report can provide policy-makers with a foundation for reviewing the current and prospective policies, to enhance and highlight the vital role and need for entrepreneurship in India. The major findings and appropriate recommendations for policy-making are highlighted under the conclusion. The findings are based on a survey of 3,317 adults sampled across the country. To ensure national representation of the population and generalisation power of findings, appropriate weights were used for age groups, gender and urban-rural classifications.

The 2020–21 GEM India report also provides a range of new information relevant to the entrepreneurship ecosystem as well. The effect of the pandemic on entrepreneurship growth in the country, is visible in this report. The detailed information is a product of the survey conducted and experts interviewed for this study in India and throughout the world, by global entrepreneurship teams. It is a result of a large survey, answering the same questions throughout the global entrepreneurship monitored participants. Every year modifications are made and new additions in the data collection are introduced. In this year too, keeping the impact of COVID-19 in mind, GEM has included new questions regarding barriers and opportunities related to the pandemic, as well as about the effects of the pandemic on household income. In this survey, the APS enquired about the impacts of the pandemic, in terms of its effects on the ease (or difficulty) of starting a venture, whether a new or existing business had to be curtailed, how growth expectations were affected, and about the adequacy (or otherwise) of government responses to the pandemic's economic impact.

In this report, it is observed that the pandemic has negatively affected business and entrepreneurship in most of the countries. The impact can be seen in India as well. The enabling factors in the country have dropped in percentage from last year. However, not all the factors have been affected adversely. The perceived opportunity has not been much affected. It indicates that youth are still confident that opportunities are available in their area. Moreover, about 81 of the youth of the country, believe that they possess the knowledge and skills to start their career in entrepreneurship. Fear of failure among youth has increased by 1 percent and about 56 percent of the people reported that they have fear failure for starting a new business. A significant impact can be seen on the entrepreneurial intention of the individuals. There has been a 39 percent change and only 20 percent of the youth have an intention to become entrepreneurs, even if they possess the capability and there are opportunities in the country as well. The expectation to start a new business has also gone down and about 22 percent of the youth expects to start a new business in the next 3 years.

Although the impact of the pandemic has a mixed effect on enabling factors, however, it has affected every aspect of the entrepreneurship activity in the countries (see fig 5.1). Nascent entrepreneurship is decreased from last year's 9.44% to 3.17% in 2020-21. There has been a 66 percent change downwards. Another important variable, new entrepreneur rate is also decreased from 5.90 to 2.27 in 2020-21. The data figure also shows a high decrease in Total entrepreneurial activity from last year. The change has been recorded at 64 percent decreasing from 15 percent in 2019-20 to 5.34 percent in 2020-21. Another important aspect of entrepreneurial activity is male versus female entrepreneurial activity. In the case of males, total entrepreneurial activity has decreased by 53 while in the case of females it is decreased by 79 percent. The data also indicates that businesses that are 42 months older have also decreased by 50%.

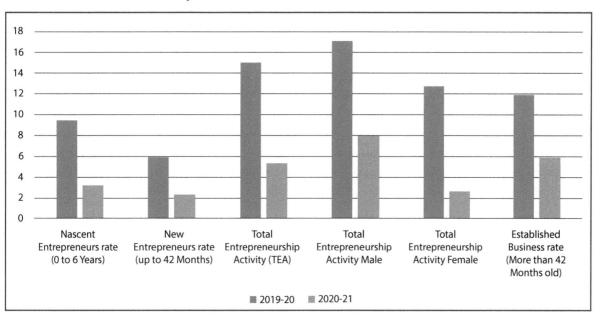

Figure 5.1   Change in the entrepreneurial activity due to pandemic
Source: *APS Survey 2020-21*

5.1 KEY POINTS FROM THE ADULT POPULATION SURVEY (APS)

❏   There are a large number of youths, who positively answered the 'know someone who has started a new business'. The data highlights, that around 62% of the youth have reported, that they know someone who has started a business recently.

❏   The results show that 82% of the population perceives, that there is a good opportunity to start a business in their area. Of the 47 economies, which participated, India has ranked 3rd for perceived opportunities.

❏   About 82% of the youth believe, they possess the skills and knowledge to start a business. The statistics have marginally decreased from last year. The data for 2012–20, highlighted that 85% of the youth have reported that they have desirable skills to start the business.

❏   The data shows that fear of failure has increased by 1 percent among youth. It was 56% in 2019-20 whereas, it has increased to 57% for 2020-21. The data highlights that there is a fear of failure among youth to choose and to be entrepreneurs.

❏   Entrepreneurial intention is a very important part of the GEM research, which highlights the possibility of youth getting into the business. The level of intentions among the population, keeps changing and compared to the last year's survey, a significant negative change has been observed. Entrepreneurial intentions had been 33.3% in 2019–20 which fell to 20.31% in 2020–21. This negative change of perception may be due to the lockdown and impact of the COVID 19 Pandemic.

❏   The rate of total early-stage entrepreneurship (TEA) in India, has also been severely affected by the pandemic and it came down to 5.34 percent from last year's 15%. The finding is also in line with other economic parameters of the country. The change has been observed at 64 percent decreased from 15 percent in 2019-20.

❑ The findings reveal that pandemic has negatively impacted Total Entrepreneurial Activities (TEA) in the country. However, it is more severe in case of the female youth. Female entrepreneurial activities have decreased by 79 percent, while male entrepreneurial activities have decreased by 53 percent.

❑ The observation for established business ownership is important and it is found that 5.88% of youth have reported that they are engaged in an established business. The numbers decreased by 51 percent from last year's 11.92%.

❑ An important finding of this survey is that 53 percent of Indians reported that they know someone who started a new business and a slightly high proportion, 60 percent of the youth perceived that they know someone who stopped a business during a pandemic. It is also important to mention here, that more than 84 percent of the youth in India, reported that the pandemic has delayed the business operations in the country.

❑ An effort has also been made to understand the impact of pandemics on household income. The results presented in this report indicate that pandemic has a very negative impact on household income. In India, about 44 percent of youth have perceived that pandemic harms their household income.

5.2 KEY POINTS FROM THE NATIONAL EXPERT SURVEY (NES)

❑ Out of the low-income economies (India, Angola, Burkina Faso, Togo and Morocco), India has been tremendously good as an entrepreneurial ecosystem. India is a leading ecosystem for entrepreneurs, as compared to the other low-income economies, across all pillars of framework conditions.

❑ Across a couple of the government-related Framework Conditions, India did better in 2020, than it did in 2019. This improvement in institutional support for entrepreneurship is reflected in the experts' assessment of the government's response to the pandemic, where India's 6.6 score, places it fifth, among all GEM participating economies.

❑ Experts scored the entrepreneurial response at 7.0 (10th among all GEM participating economies). This reflects a reasonably strong estimation of how entrepreneurs weathered the challenges of 2020.

❑ *Entrepreneurial Finance:* The financial ecosystem for entrepreneurs is highly favourable in the country. Every year, the country is putting a lot of resources to strongly back the financial ecosystem of the country. In National Expert Survey, experts gave India a 6.4 score on 'Access to entrepreneurial finance', highest amongst all GEM participating economies. This score is higher than previous year's score (2019 score was 5.7).

❑ *Government Policy & Programme:* For 'Government policy: taxes and bureaucracy', experts scored the economy at 5.7 in 2020 (sixth among the GEM participating economies), up from 5.1 in 2019, while for 'Government entrepreneurship programs', India scored 5.8 in 2020 (11th among GEM participating economies), compared to 5.1 in 2019. Overall, government programmes are doing very well in providing a favourable ecosystem to the entrepreneurs. Most importantly, there is adequate count of government programmes, along with the support from business incubators and science parks.

❑ *Entrepreneurial Education:* India stands at rank 6th (Entrepreneurship Education in Schools) and 14th (Entrepreneurship Education in Post Schools) among other GEM participating Countries.

❑ *The Commercial and legal infrastructure* is improved in the country. As compared to last year, this year we can observe a considerable rise in the rank. Country has 6th rank now, which was 8th in 2020 globally.

❑ *Physical Infrastructure in India:* Out of all framework conditions, this is one of outperforming EFC in Indian entrepreneurial ecosystem. All dimensions of this condition are equally favourable for entrepreneurs. Current rank in this EFC is 16th which was 29th during previous year.

- ❏ *Research and Development:* Research and development of the nation creates commercial opportunities for the entrepreneurs. The overall strength of this framework condition is normally good. Current rank of this EFC is 3rd which was 6th during previous year.
- ❏ *Social and Cultural Norms in India:* This framework condition is contributing very well in making of the country's favourable ecosystem for the entrepreneurs. There has been improvement in the rank. Current rank of this EFC is 8th, which was 12th during previous year.

5.3 NATIONAL ENTREPRENEURSHIP CONTEXT INDEX

Global Entrepreneurship Monitor's National Entrepreneurship Context Index (GEM NECI) provides policymakers with insights, on how to foster such an environment. The NECI summarises the assessment of Entrepreneurship Framework Conditions into a single composite score of the ease of starting and developing a business. The index measures the 12 Entrepreneurial Environment Conditions (EFCs) that make up the context in which entrepreneurial activity takes place in a country.

In its latest ranking, Indonesia, Netherlands, Taiwan and India are the top four.

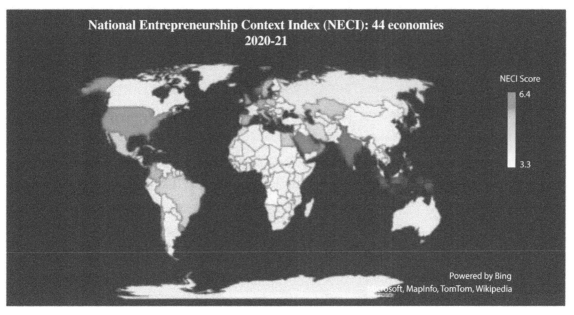

Figure 5.2   National Entrepreneurship Context Index 2020-21
Source: NES Survey 2020-21

5.4 POLICY SUGGESTIONS

The Entrepreneurship Education at both, school and post school levels, need push, so as to create a cadre of youth who would be aspiring for entrepreneurial career. There is a need to induct entrepreneurship related courses - at school as well as higher learning campuses - so that academic institutions could help create young and creative minds, who could join the country's endeavours towards development of entrepreneurship and start-ups.

The Research and development have always strengthened in building favourable climate for entrepreneurship in a country. The Government of India's initiatives in this area have yield lots of new patents and commercialisation of technology. This sector further needs support so as to create technology-based opportunities for aspiring and students' entrepreneurs.

Research and Policy Advocacy in the field of entrepreneurship and business is the need of the hour. Institutions of higher learning, may join hands and put efforts in decoding the existing polices, in the light of global market and customer demands. This will open-up new avenues for the country to go global and forge linkages for Small and Medium Enterprises to collaborate for businesses outside the country.

Further, there is a need to create pool of business mentors, who would support emerging start-ups and entrepreneurs, in order to achieve sustainability. Also, to strengthen the initiative of 'Vocal for Local', it is desired to streamline value chains of indigenously manufactured goods and services. The country has learned that local entrepreneurs have supported mankind in big ways during the pandemic and hence, it is suggested to develop a system through which these local entrepreneurs could join the larger part of value chain and get a better business market from rest of the country's markets.

5.5 HIGHLIGHTS

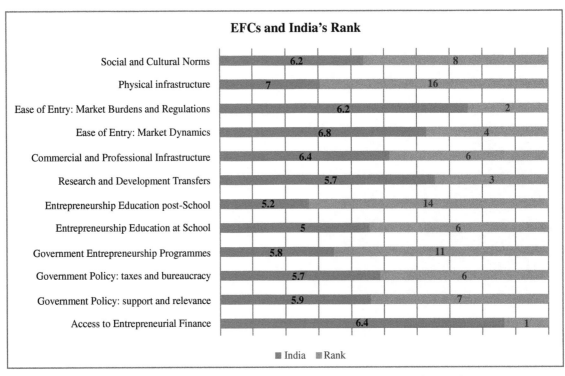

Figure 5.3   Entrepreneurial Framework Conditions (EFCs) and India's Rank
Source: NES Survey 2020-21

Factors which are enabling, fostering and restricting entrepreneurship development in the country:

Table 5.1   Constraints in Enhancing Entrepreneurial Activity

SN	Factors	Percentage
1	Cultural and Social Norms	55.6
2	Education and Training	44.5
3	Capacity for Entrepreneurship	35.5
4	Access to Physical Infrastructure	33.3
5	Financial Support	26.7

Source: NES Survey 2020-21

Table 5.2   Fostering Factors to Enhance Entrepreneurial Activity

SN	Factors	Percentage
1	Cultural and Social Norms	53.4
	Government Policies	51.1
2	Access to Physical Infrastructure	44.5
3	Capacity for Entrepreneurship	35.5
4	Perceived Population Composition	31.0
5	Economic Climate	22.3

Source: *NES Survey 2020-21*

Table 5.3   Recommendations to Enhance Entrepreneurial Activity

SN	Factors	Percentage
1	Education and Training	80.1
2	Government Programs	26.7
3	Economic Climate	26.7
4	Government Policies	26.7
5	Cultural and Social Norms	26.7

Source: *NES Survey 2020-21*

GEM Project: Overview

GEM research project is a revolutionary effort at assessing the levels of entrepreneurial activity prevalent in different nations of the world, and linking them to the entrepreneurial framework conditions of the country on the one hand and projected economic growth on the other. The project was initiated in 1999 by the London Business School, UK, and Babson College, USA, and is being carried out year after year since then. In last report about 50+ countries have participated in the project. Today, Global Entrepreneurship Monitor (GEM) has emerged as the world's leading entrepreneurship study and is the richest platform of entrepreneurship research.

GEM studies the behaviour of individuals who start their own business. The study provides a more detailed picture of entrepreneurial activity than what is depicted in official national registry data sets.

GEM started in 1997, and has examined more than 100 economies from every corner of the globe since then. GEM appears regularly in major international media outlets such as the Wall Street Journal, The Economist and The Financial Times.

GEM PROJECT IN INDIA

The prestigious GEM Research Project was initiated in India by the N.S. Raghavan Centre for Entrepreneurial Learning (NSRCEL) at IIM-Bangalore in 2001. Following the successful accomplishment of GEM India research project 2001, it was again undertaken in 2002. Back then, the GEM Research model was in its nascent stage and the 'Assessment of Entrepreneurial Activity' in the country was a new concept. Prof. Mathew J. Manimala (NSRCEL-IIM-B) conducted GEM India survey during 2001 and 2002 under GEM Research Project; and delivered research work in the form of two annual reports. Subsequently during 2006-08 a team of Prof. I.M. Pandey, Prof. Ashutosh Bhupatkar and Prof. Janki Raman from the Pearl School of Business-Gurgaon conducted GEM India study. The surveys were conducted over three years and the data featured in GEM Global Report 2006, 2007 and 2008. However, the GEM India team could not publish the National Report during the same period. In the succeeding years (2008-2011) GEM India study was not undertaken.

In 2011, with an aim to continue with the GEM India Study, three institutions i.e. Entrepreneurship Development Institute of India-Ahmedabad, Wadhwani Centre for Entrepreneurship Development, Indian School of Business, Hyderabad and Institute of Management Technology-Ghaziabad formed the GEM India Consortium 2012-15.

The 'GEM India' consortium conducted research studies during 2012, 2013 and 2014. 'The research results conducted in 2013, featured in the GEM National Report-2013 and GEM National Report-2014.

After three years, 'GEM India 2012-15' consortium was reconstituted. The three institutions (i.e. EDII-Ahmedabad, Jammu and Kashmir Entrepreneurship Development Institute of India-JKEDI and Centre for Entrepreneurship Development Madhya Pradesh-CEDMAP) agreed to conduct the GEM study in a time-bound manner, to suit GEM Global schedule. This team could produce GEM India National Reports 2015/16, 2016/17, 2017/18. EDII-Ahmedabad produced the 2019/20 GEM Report, independently.

The present 'GEM India Team' comprises Entrepreneurship Development Institute of India which is the Lead Institution and the Secretariat of the GEM India Team. Prof. Sunil Shukla (Director General, EDII) is the National Team Leader for GEM India Study.

PUBLISHED GEM INDIA REPORTS

Entrepreneurship Development Institute of India, Ahmedabad

The Entrepreneurship Development Institute of India (EDII), Ahmedabad was set up in 1983 as an autonomous and not-for-profit Institute with support of apex financial institutions - the IDBI Bank Ltd., IFCI Ltd., ICICI Bank Ltd. and State Bank of India (SBI). The Government of Gujarat pledged twenty-three acres of land on which stands the majestic and sprawling EDII Campus. EDII began by conceptualising Entrepreneurship Development Programmes (EDPs), and subsequently launched a fine tuned and tested training model for New Enterprise Creation, popularly known today as EDII-EDP model. Gradually EDII moved on to adopt the role of a National Resource Institute in the field, broadbasing its efforts internationally too, with the setting up of Entrepreneurship Development Centres in Cambodia, Laos, Myanmar, Vietnam and Uzbekistan. EDII works with the Central Government and various State Governments in a collaborative frame. The Institute plays a major role in creating and sharpening the entrepreneurial culture in Gujarat and the country.

It conducts a variety of programmes and projects across sectors under its in-house Departments of Policy Advocacy, Knowledge and Research, Entrepreneurship Education; Projects; Business Development Services & National Outreach and Developing Economy Engagement. Emphasizing on Research, EDII also set up the Centre for Research in Entrepreneurship Education and Development (CREED) on its campus, in the year 1997. The goal of CREED is to facilitate expansion of the boundaries of knowledge and give an identifiable thrust to the Entrepreneurship Development Movement. The focus areas of CREED include Entrepreneurship Education, Innovations in Training Techniques, Voluntary Sector: Issues and Interventions, Gender and Enterprise Development, Micro Finance and Micro Enterprise Development and Emerging Profile of Entrepreneurship.

In consonance with the emphasis on startups and innovations, EDII has hosted the Technology Business Incubator, CrAdLE. The TBI is catalyzed and supported by DST, Govt. of India. It focusses on incubating start-ups in the potential areas of food/agriculture, manufacturing, renewable energy and healthcare.

The first national resource institute in entrepreneurship training, research, education and institution building, EDII has successfully brought about a change in the way entrepreneurship is perceived. The Institute has earned regional, national and international recognition for boosting entrepreneurship and start-ups across segments and sectors through innovative models and by intermediating creatively among stakeholders such as; new age potential entrepreneurs, existing entrepreneurs, incubation centres, and venture capitalists.

THE DEPARTMENTS AT EDII

Policy Advocacy, Knowledge and Research

An Acknowledged Centre for Research in Entrepreneurship, Public Policy & Advocacy, this Department seeks to provide conceptual underpinnings to national and international policies, assist policy makers in their efforts to promote entrepreneurship opportunities and call upon government bodies and private organizations to integrate entrepreneurship in their development policies.

Entrepreneurship Education

To augment the supply of new entrepreneurs, this Department aims at establishing entrepreneurship as an academic discipline and creating a conducive ecosystem for its growth. The Department offers industry relevant approved academic courses and programmes to strengthen entrepreneurship education, and undertakes curriculum development on entrepreneurship, thus establishing higher-order achievements in the domain.

Department of Projects

Towards undertaking projects for economic and entrepreneurial transformations, this Department works for the Corporates as well as the Government. The Department aims at partnering with Government to implement innovation-led projects, institutionalizing S & T entrepreneurship in academic and specialized institutions, developing and enhancing skills of potential/existing entrepreneurs in emerging sectors such as agriculture, food processing, handlooms, tourism, etc. and collaborating with corporates to build intrapreneurial skills.

Business Development Services and National Outreach

Considering the significance of fostering global competitiveness and growth of Micro, Small & Medium Enterprises (MSMEs), this Department targets providing business development services across regions and sectors, accelerating start-ups, facilitating growth of existing MSMEs and catering to the requirements of MSMEs across the country

Developing Economy Engagement

In order to facilitate developing countries to establish a flourishing entrepreneurial eco-system, this Department aims at institutionalizing entrepreneurship development initiatives in developing countries, sensitizing stakeholders in the entrepreneurial eco-system in the developing economies about the ways and means of promoting and sustaining MSMEs and training and skilling to ensure human resource development.

Appendix

Table A1   Impact of the pandemic on household income, GEM 2020: percentage of adults aged 18-64

	Strongly decrease	Somewhat decrease	No substantial change	Somewhat increase	Strongly increase
Angola	54.4	29.7	11.5	3.4	1.1
Austria	7.4	24.9	60.8	6.4	0.5
Brazil	31.1	32.1	30.0	5.5	1.3
Burkina Faso	39.1	34.0	26.3	0.5	0.1
Canada	11.9	29.9	48.2	7.5	2.5
Chile	43.5	30.0	23.5	1.8	1.2
Colombia	42.2	36.4	15.0	2.8	3.6
Croatia	12.8	26.9	43.3	14.7	2.3
Cyprus	17.1	26.6	54.8	1.2	0.3
Egypt	47.2	34.0	16.2	1.6	1.0
Germany	8.2	21.5	63.1	5.9	1.3
Greece	26.0	29.1	43.9	0.7	0.3
Guatemala	34.8	37.0	23.2	3.2	1.8
India	43.5	42.3	10.7	3.4	0.2
Indonesia	22.7	57.4	18.5	1.1	0.2
Iran	14.6	36.8	46.9	1.7	0.1
Israel	0.0	42.2	24.6	30.1	3.1
Italy	12.3	39.4	47.3	1.0	0.0
Kazakhstan	37.0	55.6	7.4	0.0	0.0
Kuwait	23.3	31.1	37.3	5.2	3.1
Latvia	12.4	23.7	61.7	1.7	0.4
Luxembourg	6.5	19.8	68.8	4.4	0.5
Morocco	40.7	30.2	28.8	0.3	0.0
Netherlands	6.5	15.0	74.0	3.6	0.9
Norway	3.6	15.2	72.7	7.4	1.1
Oman	16.1	31.5	50.2	1.5	0.7
Panama	48.9	29.7	18.7	1.3	1.4
Poland	21.7	33.9	42.2	2.0	0.2
Qatar	18.3	33.1	47.4	0.7	0.4

	Strongly decrease	Somewhat decrease	No substantial change	Somewhat increase	Strongly increase
Republic of Korea	1.9	32.1	46.5	19.4	0.0
Russian Federation	19.2	42.0	36.3	2.0	0.5
Saudi Arabia	20.5	50.5	27.0	1.8	0.2
Slovak Republic	12.5	38.0	45.9	2.9	0.8
Slovenia	10.5	34.2	48.6	6.2	0.5
Spain	15.6	27.1	55.1	1.9	0.2
Sweden	4.6	19.1	66.7	8.0	1.6
Switzerland	10.2	29.8	56.9	2.8	0.3
Taiwan	16.7	23.1	58.6	1.0	0.5
Togo	74.6	15.2	9.6	0.4	0.2
United Arab Emirates	20.3	47.8	28.2	2.1	1.7
United Kingdom	13.2	25.3	56.3	4.2	1.1
United States	16.2	23.4	49.8	7.6	3.0
Uruguay	29.8	32.3	34.3	2.4	1.3

Table A2 Entrepreneurial activity, GEM 2020: percentage of adults aged 18–64
An equals sign (=) indicates that the ranking position is tied with another economy or economies

	Region	Average income level	Nascent entrepreneurship rate	
			Score	Rank/43
Angola	Midde East & Africa	Low	27.3	1
Austria	Europe & North America	High	4.1	32
Brazil	Latin America & Caribbean	Middle	10.2	16
Burkina Faso	Midde East & Africa	Low	11.5	9
Canada	Europe & North America	High	8.7	19
Chile	Latin America & Caribbean	High	19.8	4
Colombia	Latin America & Caribbean	Middle	18.0	5
Croatia	Europe & North America	High	9.1	18
Cyprus	Europe & North America	High	5.1	26=
Egypt	Midde East & Africa	Low	4.9	28
Germany	Europe & North America	High	3.1	37=
Greece	Europe & North America	High	3.3	35
Guatemala	Latin America & Caribbean	Middle	12.4	7
India	Central & East Asia	Low	3.2	36
Indonesia	Central & East Asia	Middle	2.5	40
Iran	Midde East & Africa	Middle	4.2	31
Israel	Midde East & Africa	High	5.1	26=
Italy	Europe & North America	High	0.9	43
Kazakhstan	Central & East Asia	Middle	12.1	8
Kuwait	Midde East & Africa	High	11.3	10
Latvia	Europe & North America	High	10.1	17
Luxembourg	Europe & North America	High	5.7	24
Morocco	Midde East & Africa	Low	3.0	39
Netherlands	Europe & North America	High	6.9	22
Norway	Europe & North America	High	4.7	29
Oman	Midde East & Africa	High	10.4	14=
Panama	Latin America & Caribbean	High	23.0	2
Poland	Europe & North America	High	1.6	42

New business ownership rate		Early-stage Entrepreneurial Activity (TEA)		Established Business Ownership (EBO) rate		Employee Entrepreneurial Activity (EEA)	
Score	Rank/43	Score	Rank/43	Score	Rank/43	Score	Rank/43
24.3	1	49.6	1	9.2	12	1.3	26
2.2	40	6.2	37	7.8	14	5.4	9=
13.4	4	23.4	7	8.7	13	4.5	15
12.0	5	23.0	8	12.4	5	0.3	40
7.5	11	15.6	15=	7.3	15=	5.3	11
7.2	12=	25.9	6	6.1	25=	3.2	18
14.0	3	31.1	4	5.5	30	2.1	22
3.7	29	12.7	21	4.2	36=	6.4	2=
3.6	30=	8.6	26=	7.3	15=	6.0	6=
6.7	14=	11.3	23	5.2	31	0.2	41=
1.8	41	4.8	41	6.2	24	6.4	2=
5.5	20	8.6	26=	14.6	3	1.2	27
16.4	2	28.3	5	12.3	6	1.1	28=
2.3	39	5.3	39	5.9	28=	0.1	43
7.2	12=	9.6	24	11.4	8	1.1	28=
3.8	27=	8.0	31=	14.5	4	0.8	31=
3.6	30=	8.5	28=	4.2	36=	6.1	5
1.0	43	1.9	43	2.2	43	0.7	36
8.5	10	20.1	10	4.3	35	0.9	31=
8.6	9	19.2	11	5.9	28=	6.0	6=
5.8	19	15.6	15=	11.1	9=	3.4	17
2.4	38	8.0	31=	3.6	40	4.3	16
4.1	26	7.1	36	6.8	19	0.5	38
4.9	23=	11.5	22	7.0	17=	1.7	23=
2.9	35=	7.6	34	4.1	38=	5.8	8
5.9	18	16.0	14	2.5	41=	0.8	31=
9.8	7	32.4	3	4.1	38=	2.7	19
1.5	42	3.1	42	12.2	7	0.9	31=

	Region	Average income level	Nascent entrepreneurship rate	
			Score	Rank/43
Qatar	Midde East & Africa	High	11.2	11
Republic of Korea	Central & East Asia	High	8.2	20
Russian Federation	Europe & North America	Middle	4.0	33
Saudi Arabia	Midde East & Africa	High	10.8	12
Slovak Republic	Europe & North America	High	10.4	14=
Slovenia	Europe & North America	High	3.1	37=
Spain	Europe & North America	High	2.4	41
Sweden	Europe & North America	High	4.5	30
Switzerland	Europe & North America	High	6.4	23
Taiwan	Central & East Asia	High	3.6	34
Togo	Midde East & Africa	Low	21.7	3
United Arab Emirates	Midde East & Africa	High	7.3	21
United Kingdom	Europe & North America	High	5.2	25
United States	Europe & North America	High	10.7	13
Uruguay	Latin America & Caribbean	High	15.9	6

New business ownership rate		Early-stage Entrepreneurial Activity (TEA)		Established Business Ownership (EBO) rate		Employee Entrepreneurial Activity (EEA)	
Score	Rank/43	Score	Rank/43	Score	Rank/43	Score	Rank/43
6.6	16	17.2	13	6.1	25=	6.6	1
5.0	21=	13.0	20	16.1	2	1.5	25
4.6	25	8.5	28=	4.7	34	0.4	39
6.7	14=	17.3	12	5.1	32=	1.1	28=
3.8	27=	13.9	19	6.5	22=	2.5	20
3.0	33=	6.0	38	7.0	17=	5.2	12=
2.9	35=	5.2	40	6.7	20=	0.8	31=
3.0	33=	7.3	35	6.0	27	6.2	4
3.2	32	9.2	25	6.7	20=	5.2	12=
5.0	21=	8.4	30	11.1	9=	2.3	21
11.7	6	32.9	2	17.8	1	0.6	37
8.8	8	15.4	17=	2.5	41=	1.7	23=
2.7	37	7.8	33	6.5	22=	5.4	9=
4.9	23=	15.4	17=	9.9	11	4.8	14
6.1	17	21.9	9	5.1	32=	0.2	41=

Table A3 Attitudes and perceptions in an age of COVID-19, GEM 2020
An equals sign (=) indicates that the ranking position is tied with another economy or economies

	Personally know an entrepreneur, % adults 18–64		Perceived opportunities, % adults 18–64		Perceived ease of starting a business, % adults 18–64		Perceived capabilities, % adults 18–64		Fear of failure, % of adults 18–64 seeing opportunities	
	Score	Rank/43	Score	Rank/43	Score	Rank/43	Score	Rank/43	Score	Rank/43
Angola	70.7	7	75.6	6	69.8	8=	82.3	4	34.8	35
Austria	53.9	25	31.2	36	47.5	28	53.3	31=	36.8	34
Brazil	74.2	4	57.3	15=	41.4	32	67.8	12	43.4	19
Burkina Faso	60.7	20	75.5	7	44.0	30	84.1	3	49.1	7=
Canada	51.0	28	49.1	19	67.7	14	55.6	27	52.0	5
Chile	65.8	13	46.7	26	46.1	29	71.7	10	46.3	15
Colombia	66.9	12	47.9	22	33.2	36=	64.8	15	39.5	31
Croatia	67.8	11	47.2	24=	30.7	38	75.0	7	52.1	4
Cyprus	68.1	9=	21.1	41	49.7	26	58.1	24	49.1	7=
Egypt	34.9	39	65.7	9	61.6	18	56.1	26	41.6	24=
Germany	44.4	34	36.0	34	54.4	23	47.6	36	31.0	37
Greece	32.5	41	27.9	37	25.9	41	53.3	31=	53.1	3
Guatemala	71.4	6	62.7	10	48.8	27	74.4	8	40.0	29
India	61.9	17	82.5	3	78.5	5	81.7	5	56.8	1
Indonesia	79.2	3	80.6	4	73.4	7	79.0	6	23.5	40
Iran	33.8	40	13.3	43	21.3	42	64.9	14	17.7	41
Israel	68.1	9=	25.0	40	12.3	43	37.7	42	45.0	16
Italy	30.6	43	62.2	13	78.1	6	60.8	21	28.4	38
Kazakhstan	84.3	1	44.8	27	51.1	25	63.8	18	17.5	42
Kuwait	58.2	21	62.6	11	64.5	15	63.4	19	47.8	12
Latvia	36.8	38	37.1	33	33.2	36=	55.3	28	41.6	24=
Luxembourg	45.9	31	41.9	30	63.8	16	45.7	37	42.3	23
Morocco	42.3	35	57.3	15=	53.9	24	63.4	20	38.7	32
Netherlands	60.8	19	48.8	20	82.9	3	43.6	40	38.3	33
Norway	44.7	32	57.0	17	84.1	2	41.6	41	27.4	39
Oman	84.2	2	83.8	2	67.8	13	64.5	16	42.8	20
Panama	52.6	27	47.2	24=	55.9	21	72.7	9	39.8	30

Knowing someone who has stopped a business due to the pandemic, % adults 18–64		Knowing someone who has started a business due to the pandemic, % adults 18–64		Pursue new opportunites due to pandemic, % of TEA		Starting a business is more difficult compared to a year ago, % of TEA		Pandemic has led to a delay in getting the business operational, % of TEA	
Score	Rank/43	Score	Rank/43	Score	Rank/43	Score	Rank/43	Score	Rank/43
71.4	2	62.1	4	46.0	13	77.9	5	82.6	9
24.1	36	11.9	33	36.5	24	54.6	28	65.5	27
63.7	4	52.1	9	58.3	7	59.9	23	71.4	22
28.7	33	13.9	28	8.2	42	51.2	32	76.5	11
36.8	29	21.4	21	49.4	10=	63.6	17	74.7	14=
56.5	11	55.2	5	52.9	8	77.0	6	82.8	8
52.9	13	54.6	6	62.2	4	64.5	14	74.7	14=
40.7	24	15.9	27	29.0	33	48.6	34	73.4	18
38.5	27	29.2	16	38.8	22	42.1	37	64.5	28
45.0	19	30.6	13=	35.3	25=	65.6	12	74.8	13
20.8	39	7.3	41	24.9	35	46.7	36	63.4	31
45.6	18	13.0	30	20.6	38	75.5	8	69.3	25
57.8	9	53.9	7	44.8	15	66.0	11	70.8	23
60.1	5	53.4	8	65.2	2	79.7	3	84.9	5
72.0	1	69.8	1	42.8	18	84.8	2	55.5	35
39.6	26	16.8	25	18.1	41	88.4	1	76.1	12
58.2	8	30.1	15	70.4	1	63.3	18	62.3	33
37.1	28	7.6	39.0	40.1	21	78.1	4	91.9	1
59.1	7	9.6	36	30.8	31	65.5	13	83.0	7
50.9	14	30.6	13=	60.6	5	26.4	40	86.7	4
22.7	37	7.9	38	32.9	28	11.9	43	63.7	30
17.2	42	6.3	43	30.7	32	58.6	25	67.6	26
43.5	20	16.9	24	18.2	40	72.9	9	82.4	10
25.9	34	16.0	26	41.0	20	52.5	31	53.4	37
17.8	41	7.5	40	37.8	23	29.3	39	47.6	41
66.5	3	62.4	3	60.1	6	52.7	30	89.0	3
54.1	12	63.2	2	64.1	3	62.9	19	73.7	17

	Personally know an entrepreneur, % adults 18–64		Perceived opportunities, % adults 18–64		Perceived ease of starting a business, % adults 18–64		Perceived capabilities, % adults 18–64		Fear of failure, % of adults 18–64 seeing opportunities	
	Score	Rank/43	Score	Rank/43	Score	Rank/43	Score	Rank/43	Score	Rank/43
Poland	62.7	16	51.6	18	58.9	19	60.0	22	41.2	27=
Qatar	52.6	26	72.3	8	67.9	12	68.2	11	41.3	26
Republic of Korea	39.9	36	44.6	28	33.9	35	53.0	33	13.9	43
Russian Federation	54.5	24	33.5	35	30.6	39	34.5	43	46.5	14
Saudi Arabia	57.3	23	90.5	1	91.5	1	86.4	2	51.6	6
Slovak Republic	71.9	5	40.9	31	26.0	40	56.4	25	48.7	10
Slovenia	57.9	22	42.0	29	62.0	17	59.4	23	43.8	18
Spain	37.4	37	16.5	42	34.6	34	51.9	35	53.6	2
Sweden	48.5	30	62.5	12	80.1	4	52.1	34	42.8	21
Switzerland	44.6	33	26.7	39	55.5	22	44.5	39	33.5	36
Taiwan	32.3	42	39.3	32	42.5	31	44.8	38	42.6	22
Togo	68.5	8	78.5	5	58.5	20	91.9	1	44.2	17
United Arab Emirates	65.5	14	62.1	14	69.5	10	54.7	29	47.1	13
United Kingdom	49.8	29	27.3	38	69.8	8=	54.5	30	48.3	11
United States	60.9	18	48.6	21	68.6	11	64.0	17	41.2	27=
Uruguay	63.6	15	47.3	23	39.4	33	65.6	13	48.8	9

Knowing someone who has stopped a business due to the pandemic, % adults 18–64		Knowing someone who has started a business due to the pandemic, % adults 18–64		Pursue new opportunites due to pandemic, % of TEA		Starting a business is more difficult compared to a year ago, % of TEA		Pandemic has led to a delay in getting the business operational, % of TEA	
Score	Rank/43	Score	Rank/43	Score	Rank/43	Score	Rank/43	Score	Rank/43
47.4	17	12.8	31	35.3	25=	38.3	38	64.3	29
42.7	21	23.6	18	41.9	19	58.2	27	72.3	20
34.2	30	20.8	22	7.7	43	61.6	20	48.0	40
40.0	25	13.4	29	20.5	39	58.4	26	55.1	36
57.1	10	41.6	11	52.1	9	49.7	33	91.3	2
31.9	32	20.6	23	32.0	30	53.6	29	49.4	38
25.4	35	6.4	42	32.3	29	25.9	41	44.9	43
41.8	22	12.7	32	25.5	34	71.4	10	69.5	24
17.9	40	10.5	34	34.5	27	24.4	42	46.0	42
21.6	38	9.8	35	24.2	36=	60.6	21	48.1	39
15.5	43	8.1	37	43.2	17	48.4	35	74.3	16
50.7	15	27.0	17	24.2	36=	76.3	7	84.7	6
59.5	6	40.4	12	45.6	14	64.4	15	72.7	19
32.9	31	22.1	19	49.4	10=	60.0	22	60.1	34
41.5	23	21.8	20	46.7	12	59.6	24	62.5	32
48.9	16	43.4	10	44.4	16	64.3	16	71.8	21

Table A4 Sector distribution of new entrepreneurial activity, GEM 2020: % of Total early-stage Entrepreneurial Activity (TEA)
An equals sign (=) indicates that the ranking position is tied with another economy or economies

	Business services		Consumer services		Extractive sector		Transforming sector	
	Score	Rank/43	Score	Rank/43	Score	Rank/43	Score	Rank/43
Angola	4.9	38	76.8	3	1.4	33=	16.9	33
Austria	36.6	5	48.6	25	4.7	16	10.1	42
Brazil	16.1	26	58.2	12	1.4	33=	24.4	19
Burkina Faso	2.5	42	52.4	20	17.7	3	27.4	11
Canada	26.4	14=	52.5	18=	2.8	26	18.3	29
Chile	19.7	21=	49.7	23	4.4	17=	26.1	15
Colombia	15.8	27=	59.2	11	1.0	39	24.0	20
Croatia	33.7	10	35.1	42	10.9	5	20.2	27
Cyprus	41.0	4	46.8	28	1.3	35=	10.9	41
Egypt	5.4	37	54.1	15	7.4	9	33.1	3
Germany	29.8	13	55.4	14	1.7	30	13.1	37=
Greece	17.5	23	52.5	18=	4.2	19	25.8	16
Guatemala	6.3	36	67.0	5	4.4	17=	22.4	23
India	3.5	40	78.8	2	9.3	6	8.4	43
Indonesia	3.1	41	61.4	7	7.0	10	28.6	8
Iran	24.1	17	41.8	35	7.9	8	26.2	13=
Israel	34.3	7=	47.2	27	1.2	38	17.3	32
Italy	23.4	18	39.4	40	21.7	2	15.5	35
Kazakhstan	14.3	31	56.2	13	3.4	24	26.2	13=
Kuwait	17.2	24	52.1	21	0.3	42=	30.4	6
Latvia	21.2	20	40.1	37	9.0	7	29.7	7
Luxembourg	43.6	1	43.4	31	1.3	35=	11.7	39
Morocco	8.6	35	53.3	17	6.1	12	32.0	4
Netherlands	41.2	3	45.8	30	1.5	32	11.5	40
Norway	41.8	2	36.6	41	5.3	14	16.3	34
Oman	9.5	34	63.9	6	1.8	29	24.8	18
Panama	14.6	30	61.0	8	3.7	22=	20.7	26
Poland	25.4	16	43.2	32	3.7	22=	27.6	10
Qatar	15.0	29	47.6	26	2.4	27	35.0	2

	Business services		Consumer services		Extractive sector		Transforming sector	
	Score	Rank/43	Score	Rank/43	Score	Rank/43	Score	Rank/43
Republic of Korea	19.7	21=	60.6	10	1.9	28	17.8	30
Russian Federation	17.1	25	39.5	39	4.1	20=	39.3	1
Saudi Arabia	3.9	39	82.2	1	0.8	40	13.1	37=
Slovak Republic	33.8	9	34.3	43	4.1	20=	27.8	9
Slovenia	22.7	19	40.5	36	5.9	13	31.0	5
Spain	30.8	12	46.5	29	5.1	15	17.6	31
Sweden	34.4	6	39.8	38	12.2	4	13.6	36
Switzerland	33.6	11	42.6	34	1.6	31	22.2	24
Taiwan	9.6	33	69.1	4	0.5	41	20.8	25
Togo	1.5	43	50.0	22	23.2	1	25.3	17
United Arab Emirates	15.8	27=	60.8	9	0.3	42=	23.1	22
United Kingdom	26.4	14=	49.2	24	1.3	35=	23.2	21
United States	34.3	7=	42.9	33	3.1	25	19.7	28
Uruguay	12.4	32	53.8	16	6.9	11	26.9	12

Table A5 Gender, sponsorship and informal investment, GEM 2019
An equals sign (=) indicates that the ranking position is tied with another economy or economies

	Male TEA, % of male adults 18–64		Female TEA, % of female adults 18–64		Early-stage entrepreneur with sponsored business (part-owned with employer), % of adults 18–64	
	Score	Rank/50	Score	Rank/50	Score	Rank/50
Angola	48.1	1	51.1	1	18.0	1
Austria	7.0	39	5.3	32	2.4	25
Brazil	25.6	7	21.3	8	0.4	43
Burkina Faso	24.8	8	21.5	7	1.4	36
Canada	17.3	15=	13.9	14	8.7	9=
Chile	29.9	5	22.1	6	1.5	33=
Colombia	32.2	3	30.2	3	17.2	2
Croatia	16.1	20	9.3	22	7.1	13
Cyprus	11.0	24	6.1	30	1.5	33=
Egypt	16.7	19	5.4	31	6.1	14
Germany	5.1	41	4.4	40	1.3	37=
Greece	10.6	27	6.7	27=	2.3	26=
Guatemala	31.3	4	25.5	5	1.2	39
India	7.9	37	2.6	41	3.1	23=
Indonesia	9.1	36	10.0	20	9.5	7
Iran	10.9	25=	5.1	33	1.9	31
Israel	10.4	28	6.7	27=	3.3	19=
Italy	2.9	43	0.9	43	1.3	37=
Kazakhstan	19.3	12	20.9	9	16.8	3
Kuwait	20.4	10	16.9	13	7.8	12
Latvia	20.0	11	11.2	18	2.1	30
Luxembourg	10.9	25=	4.9	34=	1.6	32
Morocco	9.8	30=	4.5	39	4.1	19=
Netherlands	13.4	23	9.6	21	5.2	15=
Norway	10.2	29	4.9	34=	0.5	42
Oman	14.7	22	17.3	12	8.7	9=
Panama	35.6	2	29.1	4	15.1	4

Early-stage entrepreneur with independent business, % of adults 18–64		Informal investment, % of adults 18–64		Median amount invested (US$) by those investing in someone else's startup and saying how much	
Score	Rank/50	Score	Rank/50	US$	Rank/50
31.6	1	12.1	4	121	42
3.8	35	4.4	19=	5,680	18=
23.0	5	6.6	10	930	34
21.5	6	6.4	11	156	41
6.9	19	4.5	17=	7,370	15
24.4	3	19.7	1	1,256	32
13.9	8	6.9	9	534	35
5.6	28	2.6	31=	301	39
7.1	17=	3.2	27=	11,360	9=
5.2	31	3.1	29=	1,565	29
3.5	37	4.0	21	5,680	18=
6.3	20=	3.1	29=	11,360	9=
27.2	2	12.9	3	390	37
2.2	40=	1.0	42	267	40
0.0	43	2.5	34	343	38
6.1	25=	2.1	36=	480	36
5.3	30	2.1	36=	14,490	5
0.7	42	0.1	43	28,400	1
3.3	38	3.2	27=	2,418	27
11.4	12	7.0	8	11,384	8
13.5	9=	3.4	24=	3,408	25
6.3	20=	5.1	13	6,057	17
3.0	39	1.8	40	1,045	33
6.3	20=	4.8	15	5,680	18=
7.1	17=	4.4	19=	10,574	11
7.3	16	2.1	36=	1,429	31
17.2	7	7.4	6	1,500	30

	Male TEA, % of male adults 18–64		Female TEA, % of female adults 18–64		Early-stage entrepreneur with sponsored business (part-owned with employer), % of adults 18–64	
	Score	Rank/50	Score	Rank/50	Score	Rank/50
Poland	3.8	42	2.4	42	0.8	41
Qatar	18.4	14	12.3	16	4.3	18
Republic of Korea	15.3	21	10.6	19	5.2	15=
Russian Federation	9.7	32=	7.3	25=	2.3	26=
Saudi Arabia	17.0	17	17.7	11	11.3	5
Slovak Republic	18.8	13	8.9	23	3.3	21=
Slovenia	7.1	38	4.8	36=	1.0	40
Spain	5.6	40	4.8	36=	1.5	33=
Sweden	9.7	32=	4.8	36=	2.2	29
Switzerland	9.8	30=	8.7	24	3.1	23=
Taiwan	9.6	34	7.3	25=	4.1	19=
Togo	29.8	6	35.6	2	9.6	6
United Arab Emirates	16.8	18	12.2	17	9.2	8
United Kingdom	9.5	35	6.2	29	2.3	26=
United States	17.3	15=	13.6	15	4.7	17
Uruguay	23.8	9	20.1	10	8.4	11

Early-stage entrepreneur with independent business, % of adults 18–64		Informal investment, % of adults 18–64		Median amount invested (US$) by those investing in someone else's startup and saying how much	
Score	Rank/50	Score	Rank/50	US$	Rank/50
2.2	40=	2.6	31=	3,825	24
12.9	11	7.3	7	19,226	4
7.8	15	2.6	31=	24,885	2
6.2	23=	3.7	23	1,671	28
6.0	27	14.2	2	6,661	16
10.6	14	4.6	16	5,680	18=
5.0	33	3.3	26	7,952	13
3.7	36	2.1	36=	5,680	18=
5.1	32	4.5	17=	3,265	26
6.1	25=	5.0	14	11,689	7
4.3	34	3.4	24=	7,601	14
23.3	4	11.0	5	87	43
6.2	23=	2.3	35	12,251	6
5.5	29	1.5	41	9,488	12
10.7	13	5.6	12	5,000	23
13.5	9=	3.9	22	23,500	3

Table A6 The age profile of new entrepreneurs and business exits, GEM 2020
An equals sign (=) indicates that the ranking position is tied with another economy or economies

| | Age profile of Total early-stage Entrepreneurial Activity (TEA), % of age group | | | | | | | | | |
| | 18–24 | | 25–34 | | 35–44 | | 45–54 | | 55–64 | |
	Score	Rank/43	Score	Rank/43	Score	Rank/39	Score	Rank/39	Score	Rank/39
Angola	54.2	1	55.4	1	45.2	1	41.3	1	37.3	1
Austria	6.9	31	10.0	32	6.8	37	5.0	37	2.8	35
Brazil	22.9	9	28.2	8	25.3	7	21.2	7	16.1	8
Burkina Faso	20.0	12	28.8	6	23.7	9	20.5	8	15.3	10
Canada	22.4	10	21.8	13	18.0	13	10.7	19	8.1	19
Chile	28.3	7	27.5	10	29.6	4	25.1	5	17.6	7
Colombia	33.1	4	37.4	3	30.2	3	28.9	3	22.0	4
Croatia	14.2	20	22.0	12	14.8	18	9.1	25	4.1	32
Cyprus	5.4	37	12.0	25	10.7	25	8.1	27=	5.0	28=
Egypt	13.0	23	11.7	27=	12.3	22	9.4	24	5.6	25
Germany	6.8	32=	6.5	40	5.6	41	4.2	39	2.4	38
Greece	18.2	16	9.7	35	7.4	34	6.1	34	2.6	37
Guatemala	32.9	5	31.4	5	27.5	5	22.4	6	15.5	9
India	4.2	40	6.6	39	5.8	39	4.6	38	4.6	30
Indonesia	6.8	32=	13.3	22	11.2	24	8.1	27=	5.7	24
Iran	9.4	27	11.7	27=	8.3	30=	2.6	42	3.0	34
Israel	6.4	34=	9.6	36	10.3	26	9.6	22=	5.0	28=
Italy	3.6	41	1.5	43	3.3	43	1.1	43	1.0	42
Kazakhstan	18.7	14	20.1	14	23.3	10	11.7	17	27.1	3
Kuwait	29.1	6	22.5	11	16.5	14	14.9	12	10.6	14
Latvia	25.6	8	28.4	7	16.0	16	9.6	22=	3.8	33
Luxembourg	8.3	28	9.8	33=	8.3	30=	7.7	29=	5.4	26
Morocco	5.3	38	11.6	30	7.3	35	6.3	33	1.6	41
Netherlands	11.4	24	16.5	21	11.4	23	10.2	20	8.4	17
Norway	8.1	29	8.0	37	7.1	36	7.7	29=	7.4	21=
Oman	18.1	17	18.2	20	14.1	20	13.7	14	9.0	15=

Exited a business in past year, % adults 18–64		Exited a business in past year, business continued, % adults 18–64		Exited a business in past year, business did not continue, % adults 18–64		Reason for exit, % of adults 18–64					
						Positive		Negative, not including COVID-19 pandemic		COVID-19 pandemic	
Score	Rank/39	Score	Rank/39	Score	Rank/39	Score	Rank/39	Score	Rank/39	Score	Rank/39
38.7	1	8.9	1	29.8	1	3.4	1	25.3	1	10.0	1
2.7	35=	0.6	36=	2.1	34	–	–	–	–	–	–
11.5	5	2.1	11=	9.4	4	1.0	10	6.0	4	4.5	7
4.2	24	1.0	25=	3.1	23=	0.3	33=	3.3	16	0.6	26
8.6	13	3.0	5	5.6	14=	2.3	2	4.5	9	1.7	18=
8.7	11=	0.8	31=	7.9	8	0.6	20=	3.1	20=	5.0	5
8.7	11=	2.9	6	5.8	13	1.5	4	3.1	20=	4.0	8
4.5	22=	1.6	14=	2.9	26	–	–	–	–	–	–
3.2	30	1.0	25=	2.2	31=	0.5	27=	1.3	31=	1.4	20
11.2	6	2.4	9=	8.8	6	–	–	–	–	–	–
2.0	38=	0.7	33=	1.4	37=	0.5	27=	1.3	31=	0.2	32=
3.1	31=	0.9	29=	2.2	31=	0.5	27=	1.9	26	0.7	24=
8.0	15	1.2	21=	6.8	10	0.5	27=	4.7	6=	2.8	11
4.7	21	1.0	25=	3.7	19=	0.2	37=	1.7	27=	2.9	10
4.5	22=	0.8	31=	3.7	19=	–	–	–	–	–	–
4.1	25=	1.0	25=	3.2	22	0.7	14=	3.4	14=	0.0	39
4.1	25=	1.1	24	3.0	25	0.6	20=	3.4	14=	0.2	32=
0.5	43	0.2	43	0.3	43	0.1	39	0.4	39	0.1	37=
16.7	2	1.3	20	15.4	2	0.8	12=	13.5	2	2.3	14
12.4	4	3.2	4	9.2	5	0.7	14=	4.2	12	7.4	3
3.0	33=	1.2	21=	1.9	35=	0.5	27=	2.1	25	0.4	27=
2.6	37	0.7	33=	1.9	35=	1.4	5=	0.9	35	0.3	29=
6.0	18	0.4	39=	5.6	14=	0.3	33=	4.4	10	1.2	21
5.1	20	1.6	14=	3.5	21	1.6	3	2.7	22	0.8	23
2.0	38=	0.7	33=	1.3	39	0.6	20=	1.3	31=	0.1	37=
10.8	7	2.7	7	8.1	7	1.4	5=	7.6	3	1.8	17

	Age profile of Total early-stage Entrepreneurial Activity (TEA), % of age group									
	18–24		25–34		35–44		45–54		55–64	
	Score	Rank/43	Score	Rank/43	Score	Rank/39	Score	Rank/39	Score	Rank/39
Panama	34.5	3	34.6	4	37.2	2	30.0	2	20.8	5
Poland	1.1	43	5.1	41	4.3	42	3.0	41	0.6	43
Qatar	15.3	18	19.5	16	14.9	17	16.3	10	18.3	6
Republic of Korea	7.1	30	12.4	24	16.4	15	13.0	15	13.5	12
Russian Federation	14.1	21	11.8	26	8.1	32	8.9	26	2.2	39=
Saudi Arabia	13.7	22	19.6	15	19.5	11	14.6	13	14.1	11
Slovak Republic	19.4	13	19.1	17	14.6	19	12.0	16	5.3	27
Slovenia	3.2	42	11.7	27=	8.4	29	3.6	40	2.2	39=
Spain	4.5	39	5.0	42	6.2	38	5.3	36	4.3	31
Sweden	10.0	25	9.8	33=	5.7	40	5.7	35	5.8	23
Switzerland	6.0	36	7.9	38	10.1	27	11.5	18	9.0	15=
Taiwan	6.4	34=	10.7	31	9.9	28	6.8	31	7.6	20
Togo	34.9	2	38.6	2	27.3	6	25.8	4	31.1	2
United Arab Emirates	18.4	15	18.3	19	12.9	21	10.0	21	7.4	21=
United Kingdom	9.7	26	12.6	23	8.0	33	6.4	32	2.7	36
United States	15.1	19	18.5	18	19.4	12	15.2	11	8.2	18
Uruguay	21.2	11	28.0	9	24.3	8	20.1	9	12.6	13

Exited a business in past year, % adults 18–64		Exited a business in past year, business continued, % adults 18–64		Exited a business in past year, business did not continue, % adults 18–64		Reason for exit, % of adults 18–64					
						Positive		Negative, not including COVID-19 pandemic		COVID-19 pandemic	
Score	Rank/39	Score	Rank/39	Score	Rank/39	Score	Rank/39	Score	Rank/39	Score	Rank/39
12.9	3	2.4	9=	10.6	3	0.6	20=	4.1	13	8.2	2
3.4	28	0.6	36=	2.8	27	0.6	20=	1.0	34	1.7	18=
7.7	16	1.4	18=	6.3	11=	0.7	14=	4.6	8	2.4	13
3.7	27	1.4	18=	2.4	28	0.3	33=	3.2	17=	0.3	29=
3.3	29	1.2	21=	2.2	31=	0.7	14=	1.7	27=	0.9	22
9.2	10	3.7	3	5.6	14=	1.3	7	2.3	23	5.6	4
5.8	19	2.6	8	3.1	23=	0.7	14=	3.2	17=	1.9	16
1.6	40	0.5	38	1.1	41	0.6	20=	0.8	36=	0.2	32=
1.3	42	0.3	41	1.0	42	0.2	37=	0.8	36=	0.2	32=
3.1	31=	0.9	29=	2.3	29=	1.1	9	1.7	27=	0.3	29=
1.5	41	0.2	42	1.2	40	0.3	33=	0.8	36=	0.4	27=
3.0	33=	1.6	14=	1.4	37=	0.7	14=	2.2	24	0.2	32=
9.3	9	1.6	14=	7.8	9	0.5	27=	4.3	11	4.6	6
9.6	8	5.0	2	4.6	17	1.2	8	4.8	5	3.7	9
2.7	35=	0.4	39=	2.3	29=	0.6	20=	1.4	30	0.7	24=
6.1	17	1.7	13	4.4	18	0.8	12=	3.2	17=	2.1	15
8.4	14	2.1	11=	6.3	11=	0.9	11	4.7	6=	2.7	12

Table A7 Expectations and scope, GEM 2020: % adults aged 18–64
An equals sign (=) indicates that the ranking position is tied with another economy or economies

| | Job creation expectations | | | | | |
| | 0 jobs | | 1–5 jobs | | 6 or more jobs | |
	Score	Rank/43	Score	Rank/43	Score	Rank/43
Angola	17.2	1	16.0	3=	16.4	2
Austria	3.8	23	2.3	32=	0.0	42=
Brazil	7.0	8	8.0	9	8.4	9
Burkina Faso	1.9	40	16.8	2	4.3	15
Canada	9.0	5	4.0	18	2.6	24
Chile	3.4	29=	13.3	6	9.2	8
Colombia	3.6	27=	10.7	7	16.8	1
Croatia	5.7	13	4.2	17	2.7	22=
Cyprus	2.0	36=	3.8	19=	2.8	21
Egypt	3.7	24=	3.8	19=	3.7	19=
Germany	2.2	35	1.4	41	1.2	34
Greece	4.8	17	2.7	28=	1.1	35=
Guatemala	6.0	11=	16.0	3=	6.3	10
India	2.0	36=	2.5	31	0.9	37=
Indonesia	6.3	9	3.0	25	0.3	41
Iran	3.3	31	3.4	23	1.3	32=
Israel	5.3	15=	1.7	40	1.5	27=
Italy	1.2	42	0.7	43	0.0	42=
Kazakhstan	9.4	4	5.2	12	5.5	11
Kuwait	5.5	14	4.3	16	9.5	6
Latvia	6.2	10	4.7	14	4.6	13=
Luxembourg	2.7	33	2.6	30	2.7	22=
Morocco	3.6	27=	2.1	34=	1.4	31
Netherlands	7.1	7	2.8	26=	1.5	27=
Norway	3.4	29=	2.0	37	2.2	25
Oman	10.8	2	3.7	22	1.5	27=
Panama	4.0	19=	14.4	5	13.9	3
Poland	1.1	43	1.3	42	0.7	39

At least national scope for its customers and new products or processes		Global scope for its customers and new products or processes		Expecting 25% or more of revenue from customers outside own economy	
Score	Rank/43	Score	Rank/43	Score	Rank/43
1.7	18	0.2	26=	0.6	25=
1.1	24=	0.5	15=	0.9	20=
1.1	24=	0.1	30=	0.3	35=
0.7	31=	0.2	26=	1.0	18=
3.6	6	1.3	1=	3.5	1
2.6	9	0.3	21=	0.4	31=
5.1	4	1.3	1=	2.2	7=
2.3	11=	0.7	12=	2.6	4
2.4	10	0.7	12=	2.4	5
0.7	31=	0.0	36=	0.4	31=
0.8	27=	0.3	21=	0.6	25=
1.6	19	0.5	15=	1.4	14=
0.9	27=	0.1	30=	0.5	28=
0.1	42=	0.0	36=	0.0	41=
0.3	41	0.0	36=	0.2	37=
0.4	36=	0.1	30=	0.2	37=
1.2	22=	0.3	21=	0.9	20=
0.5	34=	0.0	36=	0.1	40
0.1	42=	0.0	36=	0.0	41=
6.0	3	0.9	6=	2.3	6
2.1	14	0.8	8=	3.1	2
2.3	11=	0.4	18=	2.2	7=
0.4	36=	0.1	30=	0.2	37=
2.7	8	0.8	8=	2.0	11
1.5	20	0.6	14.0	1.0	18=
0.7	31=	0.0	36=	0.4	31=
7.0	2	1.1	5.0	2.1	10
0.4	36=	0.0	36=	0.0	41=

| | Job creation expectations | | | | | |
| | 0 jobs | | 1–5 jobs | | 6 or more jobs | |
	Score	Rank/43	Score	Rank/43	Score	Rank/43
Qatar	3.7	24=	2.1	34=	11.4	4
Republic of Korea	4.0	19=	5.0	13	4.0	17=
Russian Federation	2.0	36=	2.8	26=	3.7	19=
Saudi Arabia	2.0	36=	5.8	11	9.4	7
Slovak Republic	6.0	11=	3.8	19=	4.0	17=
Slovenia	2.6	34	1.9	38	1.5	27=
Spain	3.0	32	1.8	39	0.5	40
Sweden	4.0	19=	2.1	34=	1.1	35=
Switzerland	3.9	22	4.5	15	0.9	37=
Taiwan	3.7	24=	2.7	28=	2.0	26
Togo	10.4	3	17.6	1	4.9	12
United Arab Emirates	1.6	41	3.2	24	10.6	5
United Kingdom	4.2	18	2.3	32=	1.3	32=
United States	5.3	15=	6.0	10	4.2	16
Uruguay	7.2	6	10.0	8	4.6	13=

At least national scope for its customers and new products or processes		Global scope for its customers and new products or processes		Expecting 25% or more of revenue from customers outside own economy	
Score	Rank/43	Score	Rank/43	Score	Rank/43
7.8	1	0.3	21=	1.8	13
2.0	15	0.4	18=	0.6	25=
0.5	34=	0.2	26=	0.7	23=
0.8	27=	0.0	36=	0.8	22
2.9	7	1.2	3=	1.9	12
1.1	24=	0.5	15=	1.2	16=
0.4	36=	0.1	30=	0.3	35=
1.2	22=	0.4	18=	1.4	14=
1.4	21	0.9	6=	1.2	16=
2.3	11=	0.8	8=	0.5	28=
0.4	36=	0.1	30=	2.2	7=
4.1	5	1.2	3=	2.9	3
0.9	27=	0.3	21=	0.7	23=
1.8	16=	0.8	8=	0.5	28=
1.8	16=	0.2	26=	0.4	31=

Table A8   The motivation to start a business, GEM 2020: % of Total early-stage Entrepreneurial Activity (TEA)
An equals sign (=) indicates that the ranking position is tied with another economy or economies

	To make a difference in the world		To build great wealth or very high income		To continue a family tradition		To earn a living because jobs are scarce	
	Score	Rank/43	Score	Rank/43	Score	Rank/43	Score	Rank/43
Angola	65.3	7	63.8	18	37.3	11	89.5	3=
Austria	39.0	25=	33.4	41	21.1	32	49.3	35
Brazil	65.6	6	57.7	22	27.4	23	81.9	9
Burkina Faso	21.4	40	76.1	10	34.0	15	79.4	12
Canada	66.5	5	64.2	17	39.5	9	66.1	25
Chile	58.4	10	53.7	26	37.1	12=	81.2	10
Colombia	62.9	8	61.7	20	37.1	12=	77.0	14
Croatia	39.0	25=	47.0	30	28.7	19	69.4	23
Cyprus	37.5	28	85.2	6	21.3	31	77.4	13
Egypt	49.2	15	62.9	19	38.1	10	54.0	31
Germany	39.8	23=	52.2	28	62.0	2	45.1	37
Greece	26.9	36	45.8	31	35.7	14	69.0	24
Guatemala	76.7	2	54.8	25	46.9	6	91.1	1
India	80.7	1	74.7	12	76.8	1	87.3	5
Indonesia	44.7	18	49.8	29	41.8	8	71.4	21=
Iran	30.1	35	88.9	3	19.0	36	64.8	26
Israel	35.6	31	71.2	13	17.5	37	53.6	32
Italy	26.6	37	95.3	1	26.5	24	82.2	8
Kazakhstan	0.4	43	94.9	2	8.6	42	40.0	39
Kuwait	40.1	22	76.0	11	30.6	18	59.6	28=
Latvia	39.8	23=	41.8	34	27.5	22	73.6	17
Luxembourg	51.1	14	40.3	37	16.6	39	44.3	38
Morocco	11.8	41	45.2	32	21.4	30	72.8	18
Netherlands	46.6	17	40.9	36	24.6	27	47.8	36
Norway	36.7	30	30.1	43	11.8	41	23.1	43
Oman	47.9	16	82.2	7	48.9	4	89.8	2
Panama	66.6	4	56.3	24	45.3	7	84.7	6
Poland	22.0	39	52.8	27	20.4	34	62.0	27

	To make a difference in the world		To build great wealth or very high income		To continue a family tradition		To earn a living because jobs are scarce	
	Score	Rank/43	Score	Rank/43	Score	Rank/43	Score	Rank/43
Qatar	37.6	27	77.5	9	27.7	21	56.6	28=
Republic of Korea	10.0	42	68.6	15	5.0	43	32.9	40
Russian Federation	24.2	38	68.7	14	16.5	40	71.4	21=
Saudi Arabia	60.8	9	86.9	4	53.2	3	89.5	3=
Slovak Republic	33.6	32	38.3	39	32.4	17	73.8	16
Slovenia	44.6	19	39.7	38	21.6	29	72.2	20
Spain	32.3	33	34.9	40	17.4	38	72.3	19
Sweden	41.5	21	42.8	33	24.2	28	28.9	42
Switzerland	42.5	20	32.5	42	20.1	35	52.0	33
Taiwan	52.5	12	57.2	23	25.6	26	32.8	41
Togo	36.9	29	85.5	5	32.6	16	84.6	7
United Arab Emirates	52.4	13	77.7	8	47.6	5	74.7	15
United Kingdom	57.6	11	59.4	21	20.7	33	54.4	30
United States	68.2	3	66.0	16	28.6	20	50.2	34
Uruguay	31.7	34	41.4	35	25.9	25	80.1	11

Table A9 National Entrepreneurship Context Index (NECI) scores, and national expert scores for response to the pandemic by entrepreneurs and governments
An equals sign (=) indicates that the ranking position is tied with another economy or economies

	NECI scores	NECI rank	Entrepreneurial response	Entrepreneurial response rank	Governmental response	Governmental response rank
Indonesia	6.39	1	6.58	23	6.13	12
Netherlands	6.34	2	6.57	24	7.05	3
Taiwan	6.06	3	7.30	7	6.72	4
United Arab Emirates	6.03	4	7.53	4	7.16	2
India	6.02	5	6.99	10	6.64	5
Norway	5.74	6	6.73	19=	6.47	8
Saudi Arabia	5.69	7	7.70	1	8.44	1
Qatar	5.67	8	6.76	17=	6.42	9
Republic of Korea	5.49	9	6.37	31	5.22	19
Switzerland	5.39	10	6.76	17=	5.92	14
Israel	5.33	11	6.82	15	3.59	37
United States	5.15	12	6.83	14	2.65	44
Oman	5.10	13	6.43	30	5.76	17
Luxembourg	5.05	14	6.48	27	6.49	7
United Kingdom	5.02	15	7.49	5	5.20	20
Germany	4.93	16	6.32	32	5.80	16
Uruguay	4.88	17	6.84	13	6.38	10
Austria	4.79	18	6.56	25	6.05	13
Spain	4.69	19	6.17	35	3.50	39
Colombia	4.64	20	6.73	19=	4.61	27
Latvia	4.64	21	6.28	34	4.53	28=
Slovenia	4.59	22	6.73	19=	4.92	24
Sweden	4.52	23	6.88	11	4.26	31
Cyprus	4.47	24	6.77	16	6.19	11
Chile	4.35	25	7.13	9	5.07	23
Kuwait	4.30	26=	6.51	26	4.07	32
Kazakhstan	4.30	26=	5.48	41	3.69	35
Greece	4.30	28	6.44	29	6.51	6

	NECI scores	NECI rank	Entrepreneurial response	Entrepreneurial response rank	Governmental response	Governmental response rank
Egypt	4.30	29	6.66	22	5.12	22
Poland	4.24	30	6.31	33	5.19	21
Brazil	4.21	31	7.44	6	3.88	33
Panama	4.21	32	7.62	2	4.69	25
Mexico	4.14	33	6.86	12	2.86	43
Slovak Republic	4.12	34	5.78	38	3.71	34
Italy	4.12	35	6.47	28	4.53	28=
Iran	3.98	36	5.50	40	3.53	38
Guatemala	3.92	37	7.54	3	3.60	36
Russian Federation	3.79	38	5.42	42	3.07	41
Morocco	3.78	39	5.53	39	4.65	26
Togo	3.78	40	5.33	43	5.66	18
Croatia	3.73	41	6.11	36	5.82	15
Puerto Rico	3.58	42	7.26	8	2.94	42
Burkina Faso	3.43	43	4.82	44	4.47	30
Angola	3.31	44	6.07	37	3.28	40

Bibliography

About Indian Economy Growth Rate & Statistics. (April 2021). India Brand Equity Foundation. https://www.ibef.org/economy/indian-economy-overview

Agarwal Palak (04 August, 2020). India is home to 21 unicorns, collectively valued at $73.2 billion: Hurun Global Unicorn List 2020. CNBC TV 18. https://www.cnbctv18.com/startup/india-is-home-to-21-unicorns-collectively-valued-at-732-billion-hurun-global-unicorn-list-2020-6538511.htm

Department For Promotion of Industry And Internal Trade. (January 2021). Ease of Doing Business In India. Ministry of Commerce and Industry.Government of India.

Department For Promotion Of Industry and Internal Trade. Startup India. The Women Entrepreneurship Platform (WEP). Ministry of Commerce and Industry. https://www.startupindia.gov.in/content/sih/en/government-schemes/Wep.html

Doing Business (2020). Comparing Regulation in 190 Economies. World Bank Group.

Doing Business India. (2020). Comparing Regulation in 190 Economies. World Bank Group.

Doing Business, Measuring Business Regulations. Ease of Doing Business in India. https://www.doingbusiness.org/en/data/exploreeconomies/india

Economic Survey 2020-21 (Volume – 1). Ministry of Finance. Government of India.

Economic Survey 2020-21 (Volume – 2). Ministry of Finance. Government of India.

Global Startup Ecosystem Index (2021). Startup Blink

Klaus Schwab, Saadia Zahidi and World Economic Forum. (2020). The Global Competitiveness Report, Special edition. How Countries are performing on the Road to Recovery. World Economic Forum.

Projected GDP Ranking. (03 June, 2021). International Monetary Fund World Economic Outlook. https://statisticstimes.com/economy/projected-world-gdp-ranking.php

Stephan Ute, ZbierowskiPrzemyslaw, Perez-Luno Ana and Klausen Anna. (March 2021). Entrepreneurship during the Covid-19 Pandemic: A global study of entrepreneurs' challenges, resilience, and well-being. King's College, London.

Top 10 Women Entrepreneurs in 2020-21 by the Indian Alert (21 May, 2021). Fortune Indian Exchange. https://www.fortuneindia.com/enterprise/top-10-women-entrepreneurs-in-2020-21-by-the-indian-alert/105491

World Competitiveness ranking. IMD. https://www.imd.org/centers/world-competitiveness-center/rankings/world-competitiveness/

Atmanirbhar Bharat Abhiyaan. National Investment Promotion & Facilitation Agency. https://www.investindia.gov.in/atmanirbhar-bharat-abhiyaan

Atmanirbhar Bharat. Part–I: Businesses including MSMEs. https://cdnbbsr.s3waas.gov.in/s3850af92f8d9903e7a4e0559a98ecc857/uploads/2020/05/2020051717.pdf

COVID Resource Section Startup India. https://www.startupindia.gov.in/content/sih/en/covid-19_resource_section.html

T-HUB in Hyderabad. COVID-19 innovation challenge in partnership with Q-City. https://t-hub.co/covid-19-innovation-challenge/#

COVID-19 Innovations Development Accelerator. C-CAMP. https://www.ccamp.res.in/covid-19-innovations-deployment-accelerator

Department for Promotion of Industry and Internal Trade. (January 2021). Ease of Doing Business in India. Ministry of *Commerce and Industry. Government of India.*

Department for Promotion of Industry and Internal Trade. Start-up India. The Women Entrepreneurship Platform (WEP). Ministry of Commerce and Industry. https://www.startupindia.gov.in/content/sih/en/government-schemes/Wep.html

Doing Business (2020). Comparing Regulation in 190 Economies. *World Bank Group.*

Doing Business India. (2020). Comparing Regulation in 190 Economies. *World Bank Group.*

Doing Business, Measuring Business Regulations. Ease of Doing Business in India. https://www.doingbusiness.org/en/data/exploreeconomies/india

Economic Survey 2020-21 (Volume – 1). *Ministry of Finance. Government of India.*

Economic Survey 2020-21 (Volume – 2). *Ministry of Finance. Government of India.*

Global Startup Ecosystem Index (2021). Startup Blink

Global Entrepreneurship Monitor. National Expert Survey. https://www.gemconsortium.org/wiki/1142

Global Entrepreneurship Monitor Global Report. https://www.gemconsortium.org/file/open?fileId=50691

Klaus Schwab, Saadia Zahidi and World Economic Forum. (2020). The Global Competitiveness Report, Special edition. How Countries are performing on the Road to Recovery. *World Economic Forum.*

Shukla, s. Bharti, P. and Dwivedi, A.K. (2021). Global Entrepreneurship Monitor India Report 2019-20. https://www.gemindiaconsortium.org/gem_news-5.html

Shukla, S., Chatwal, S, Navniit., Bharti, P., Dwivedi, A.K. Shastri, V. (2020). Global Entrepreneurship Monitor India Report 2018-19. https://gemindiaconsortium.org/reports/GEM%20India%20Report%202018-19.pdf

Shukla, S., Parray, MI., Singh, C., Bharti, P. and Dwivedi, A.K. (2019) Global Entrepreneurship Monitor. India Report 2017-18. https://www.gemconsortium.org/report/global-entrepreneurship-monitor-india-report-2017-18

Stephan Ute, ZbierowskiPrzemyslaw, Perez-Luno Ana and Klausen Anna. (March 2021). Entrepreneurship during the Covid-19 Pandemic: A global study of entrepreneurs' challenges, resilience, and well-being. King's College, London.

World Competitiveness ranking. IMD. https://www.imd.org/centers/world-competitiveness-center/rankings/world-competitiveness/

Chethna (13 July, 2020). Top Features of the Atmanirbhar Bharat Abhiyan Scheme that benefits your business. MSME News. https://www.instamojo.com/blog/top-features-of-the-atmanirbhar-bharat-abhiyan-scheme-that-benefits-your-business/

Global Entrepreneurship Monitor. National Expert Survey. https://www.gemconsortium.org/wiki/1142

Global Entrepreneurship Monitor. India Report 2019-20. https://www.gemindiaconsortium.org/gem_news-5.html

Atmanirbhar Bharat Abhiyaan. National Investment Promotion & Facilitation Agency. https://www.investindia.gov.in/atmanirbhar-bharat-abhiyaan

Atmanirbhar Bharat. Part–I: Businesses including MSMEs. https://cdnbbsr.s3waas.gov.in/s3850af92f8d9903e7a4e0559a98ecc857/uploads/2020/05/2020051717.pdf

Chethna (13 July, 2020). Top Features of the Atmanirbhar Bharat Abhiyan Scheme that benefits your business. MSME News. https://www.instamojo.com/blog/top-features-of-the-atmanirbhar-bharat-abhiyan-scheme-that-benefits-your-business/

COVID Resource Section. Startup India. https://www.startupindia.gov.in/content/sih/en/covid-19_resource_section.html

T-HUB in Hyderabad. COVID-19 innovation challenge in partnership with Q-City. https://t-hub.co/covid-19-innovation-challenge/#

COVID-19 Innovations Development Accelerator. C-CAMP. https://www.ccamp.res.in/covid-19-innovations-deployment-accelerator

Agarwal Palak (04 August, 2020). India is home to 21 unicorns, collectively valued at $73.2 billion: Hurun Global Unicorn List 2020. CNBC TV 18. https://www.cnbctv18.com/startup/india-is-home-to-21-unicorns-collectively-valued-at-732-billion-hurun-global-unicorn-list-2020-6538511.htm

About Indian Economy Growth Rate & Statistics. (April 2021). India Brand Equity Foundation. https://www.ibef.org/economy/indian-economy-overview

Top 10 Women Entrepreneurs in 2020-21 by the Indian Alert (21 May, 2021). Fortune Indian Exchange. https://www.fortuneindia.com/enterprise/top-10-women-entrepreneurs-in-2020-21-by-the-indian-alert/105491

Projected GDP Ranking. (03 June, 2021). International Monetary Fund World Economic Outlook. https://statisticstimes.com/economy/projected-world-gdp-ranking.php